LET US
Praise

LET US Praise

by

JUDSON CORNWALL

Bridge-Logos

Alachua, Florida 32615 USA

Bridge-Logos

Alachua, Florida 32615 USA

Let Us Praise
by Judson Cornwall

Copyright ©2006 by Bridge-Logos

Printed in the United States of America.

Library of Congress Catalog Card Number: 2013935005
International Standard Book Number 978-0-88270-992-5

Unless otherwise identified. Scriptures quotations are from the King James Version of the Bible.

Scripture quotations identified TAB are from the Amplified Bible. Copyright © The Lockman Foundation 1954-58, and are used by permission.

Scripture quotations identified NEB are from the New English Bible. Copyright © The Delegates of the Oxford University Press and Syndics of the Cambridge University Press 1961, 1970. Reprinted by permission.

Scripture quotations identified PHILLIPS are from the New Testament in Modern English Revised edition, J.B. Phillips, translator. Copyright © J.B.Phillips 1958, 1960, 1972. Used by permission of Macmillan Publishing Company Inc.

Scripture quotations identified RSV are from the Revised Standard Version of the Bible. Copyright © Division of Christian Education of the National Council of the Churches of Christ in the United States of America 1946, 1952 ® 1971 and 1973.

Scripture quotations identified TEV are from the Good News Bible - Old Testament: Copyright © American Bible Society 1976; New Testament: Copyright © American Bible Society 1966, 1971, 1976.

Verses marked TLB are taken from the Living Bible, Copyright ® 1971 by Tyndale House Publishers, Wheaton, Ill. Used by permission.

VP 03-26-13

CONTENTS

Let Us Praise

Preface vii

1 Presented With Praise 1

2 The Purpose of Praise 11

3 The Pattern of Praise 25

4 The Paradigms of Praise 33

5 Persons in Praise 49

6 The Pact of Praise 59

7 The Performance of Praise 79

8 Persuasions to Praise 93

9 The Power of Praise 105

10 Preventives to Praise 119

11 The Permanence of Praise 131

Appendix 137

To Eleanor Louise

wife of my youth and middle age, and the three daughters

she gave me: Dorothy—Jeannie—Justine.

The longsuffering of these women in sharing me with others

has made my ministry so much easier.

Preface

In recent years, several excellent books on praise have been published by Logos. Why another?

In ministering to pastors and people with the historic church backgrounds, I find that the nuts and bolts of the subject of praise, as a public function, is often quite foreign to them. As they have opened themselves to a fuller flow of the Holy Spirit, there is a strong inner desire to express love and adoration, but an outer rigidity that prohibits their bursting forth into praise. Although they thrill to the testimonies of others who have moved into this dimension, they feel they cannot set aside past training just because of someone else's experience, however glorious it may be.

In conferences and seminars, I have been asked repeatedly, "What is the scriptural basis for praise?" This book is an attempt to answer that question. There are over 350 scriptural quotations or references in the book. I've tried to establish that praise is not Davidic but divine, that we are not emulating man's pattern but God's.

I was ministering in Africa when Logos finally convinced me to write such a book. It has been written in airports, motel rooms, guest rooms, and on conference grounds, for it was not possible to cancel a pre-committed schedule to sit down and write. During the writing, I traveled over 80,000 miles and ministered in seven countries. May the ministry of praise that

Let Us Praise teaches find an expression in the Body of Christ that is even broader and more far-reaching than my journeys.

Praise God, from whom all blessings flow!

Praise Him, all creatures here below!

Praise Him above, ye heavenly host!

Praise Father, Son, and Holy Ghost!

1

Presented With Praise

The singer had just finished his second set of gospel songs and had laid his guitar on the chair behind the pulpit. Our musical guest of the evening was apparently going to talk for a while, to give his singing voice a rest and us a change of pace.

"I want to congratulate Pastor Cornwall and the congregation on the wonderful job they've done in converting this old barn into a church ..."

Barn? I guess that's accurate enough. It does look more like a place for hay storage than for a congregation.

"Although you're a small congregation," he continued, "you've got a beautiful atmosphere here."

Did he use the word atmosphere as a euphemism for empty parking lot? What was I doing here in this nearly deserted barn? This was a home-missions work, a place for a young, eager pioneer. This was the type of anvil on which the beginning ministries of Bible school graduates were forged and tempered. But I was no beginner—I'd been preaching more than twenty-five years, fifteen of them as a pastor. Before pastoring, I'd put in an apprenticeship under my father in two different churches and then invested another year as assistant pastor in a large church in Southern California.

"I'm impressed with the caliber of your pastor," he continued.

Freely translated, that meant he was shocked to see an experienced man in such a small church. He couldn't possibly be more shocked than I was. By denominational standards, I had been successful. An honor student in Bible college, and one of the youngest ministers ever to receive credentials in my denomination, I had stayed less than a year in my first church, dividing the next fourteen years between two others. I had not climbed to larger churches; I had produced them, conducting successful building programs without incurring large indebtedness. I had taken small, weak works and had left them large and strong. Why was I here?

"I first met your pastor when he was ministering in Yakima, Washington, some years ago ..."

I had left that church only a few months ago. Not only had we re-located the congregation and revamped their program and ministry, but I had spent three of those years teaching in a local Bible school in the mornings, and I had a radio ministry to boot. Part of that time I served as president of two ministerial groups, director of youth camps for my denomination, and organist for the adult camps. In fact, I was on so many committees and the platforms of so many denominational functions that some of my fellow ministers were openly jealous of me.

Not surprisingly, my church had one complaint against me: too much outside ministry. Yet I thoroughly enjoyed being called upon to minister outside the walls of my church, and took pride in my reputation within the denomination as a real workhorse.

"I had heard that Brother Cornwall had not only resigned

his church but had turned in his papers to the denomination, stating that he would never pastor another church ..."

The dear old denominational grapevine, transmitting such news faster than the telegraph. Well, I guessed there came a time in every preacher's ministry when the frustrations his ministry produced in his own life exceeded the fruit it produced in his congregation. A time when the challenge of his call was countered by an awareness of his inability to produce. Some said this was evidence of maturity, but, for many, it was merely the beginning of the end.

I had just faced such a confrontation with reality in Yakima. More and more I had questioned the standard by which we were measuring success, until I began to have doubts that the church could ever meet the true call of Christ in ministry. It seemed I was enmeshed in a web of near-fruitless activity, and the harder I drove myself, the less satisfaction I had. I began to doubt that the ideals of my youth could ever be accomplished. It finally got to the point where I felt that if I had been in any business other than religion, such an expenditure of energy, manpower, and finance with so little rate of return would have produced bankruptcy. And so, I had turned in my resignation.

I didn't want to give up the ministry; that had been a call of God on my life since boyhood. I simply wanted out of an area of ministry that was completely void of lasting, vital, spiritual life, even though it was being called successful.

My three years of teaching in a small Bible school had convinced me that the most effective means of producing change in the church was to reach future ministers while they were still in training. I had determined to dedicate the remaining years of my ministry to Bible school teaching. My denomination had offered me a teaching spot in their Washington school if I would get my Master's degree, so I had sent a transcript of my Bible college credits to several West Coast colleges and universities asking for information on a transfer of credits. The University of Oregon offered me the best transfer, and without hesitation, I moved my family to Eugene.

But as I went to enroll, I made a shocking discovery: to establish residency in the state, in order to avoid the double fees charged non-residents, would take six months! I took a job as a roofer. My wife and I were able to find some work for the Lord in the large downtown church of our denomination as the church pianist and organist. And, all in all, our family enjoyed the relaxed pace this change of life forced on us.

"I'm glad to see that what I heard was not true and that Brother Cornwall is, indeed, pastoring ..."

I wished he would stop talking and start singing again.

Oh, it was true enough that I had turned in my papers and refused to pastor again. But during the six months I was establishing residency, the officials of my former district nonetheless sent several delegations from various churches in Washington to invite me to present myself as a ministerial candidate to their congregations. Although these churches were all larger than the congregation I had just left, there had been no temptation to accept their offers. I had had it with pastoring.

"... and that he has been willing to step down to such a small congregation. I know God will bless him for it."

Step down? Dragged down was more like it! This small church, deeply in trouble and badly in debt, had suddenly lost its pastor, and I was simply asked to fill the pulpit for two Sundays. In the meantime, so serious was the condition of the church that the district officials had voted to close its doors, rather than try to continue ministry in that section of town.

This, of course, was of no concern to me; I was only a guest speaker on assignment.

Informed of the decision to close the work and lock the building, the congregation called a business meeting after I left the premises on my second Sunday. They decided to reject the district's decision and to continue struggling to produce a work in this growing section of the city. They unanimously—all fourteen of them—elected me to be their pastor and informed me of their action by phone about midnight.

Aroused from sleep, I had lacked the grace to keep from laughing out loud over the phone.

"I refused two good churches just this past week. What on earth makes you think I would take one like yours?"

I had never served such a small congregation, not even as a teenage pastor. I could not even remember having taught a Sunday school class that small.

"Well, won't you pray about it before making your final decision?" the spokesman asked.

"There's no need to," I replied. "I will never pastor another church as long as I live."

The shocked silence on the other end began to make me feel guilty, and so, since it seemed the only hope of getting back to bed was to agree, I finally said I would pray about it the next day, and then call him in the evening and tell him no.

Late in the afternoon of the following day, I was reminded of my promise. Since I was working alone on a shake roof, I just paused for a moment and prayed aloud: "Lord, you know I promised to pray about taking the pastorate of that little church, but I know this isn't your will for my life. Please do provide the guidance for them that they need. And I thank you for delivering me from pastoring."

I had picked up my hatchet and returned to my roofing when the Lord spoke to me by an inner voice that I knew was His. I had heard it before. *My son, I won't make you take it, but it would please Me if you did. If you will become their pastor, I will show you a safe way into My realm and My presence.*

"Oh, God, no! You can't do this to me! If I have to pastor, at least let it be something large enough to support my family. I'll not only have to work, I'll probably have to pay off their indebtedness. Besides, it would be a breach of courtesy to pastor a little church in this town now that I've been associated with the large downtown work. And what about the district officials? They voted to close that church!"

Little roofing was done in the ensuing hour, as I wrestled with God. I used every gambit, exhausted every argument. I reasoned. I pleaded, I threatened, I cajoled. He remained immovable.

Finally, I threw my shingling hatchet at the roof with such force that it cut all the way through the shakes and fell into the house as I cried, "All right! If you'll teach me new ways into your presence, I'll take that wretched little church!"

The disciples could not have experienced greater peace when Jesus calmed the storm on Galilee than I knew in the moments that followed.

My wife and daughters were amazed at my decision, although greatly relieved, for they sensed that my withdrawal from pastoring had heightened rather than calmed my frustrations.

Although I had the promise of God that He would show me a new way into His presence and kingdom, by habit patterns long ingrained, I immediately implemented all the old ways I had learned and used in past ministry. God graciously gave us some people so hungry and needy that they were willing to be led almost anywhere.

We tried the evangelistic center approach, but it did not bring us into the divine Presence.

We entered into demon exorcising long before it became popular in the Body of Christ, but after a while, this seemed to magnify the power of the devil rather than the presence of God.

We emphasized divine healing, then being filled with the Spirit. When each special emphasis failed to bring us into the realized presence of God, we would confess our error, back up, and start over in another direction.

During all this time, we kept a very heavy emphasis upon prayer. People were being saved, healed, filled with the Spirit, and delivered from bondage; homes were being re-united, and we were experiencing such growth that we had to build a new building. But we were not enjoying what I had once tasted in earlier ministry and had been promised in this one: the realized presence of the Lord.

During one week-night service, I vaguely recognized a visitor entering the auditorium during the song service. Although it was unusual for me to do so, I felt strongly led to walk down from the platform and introduce myself. He turned out to be someone I had known back in Bible college days. He had been on the missionary field in South America, and our paths had not crossed for many years.

I invited him to speak to us that evening, but he declined, pleading weariness of body. He had just arrived in town, having driven out from Chicago. He did, however, accept an invitation to testify briefly. His testimony electrified all of us. This man knew God! He was on intimate terms with Him. What excitement he created in my inner spirit! I pled with him to give us a series of services, and, in the will of the Lord, he agreed to stay for a week.

I wanted him to preach on knowing God, on talking to God, on coming into God's presence, but he insisted on teaching on praise, and not just teaching—he taught us to praise.

What a task he had! We wanted the power and the presence of God, but were fearful and very doubtful about praise. Although I was a member of a group long ago "born in the fire" and could still remember extended, ardent, praise sessions as a boy, I, too, had departed from this and did not know that anyone in the world was deeply involved in vocal, united, congregational praise. Our own congregational praise was generally limited to a stilted, "Praise the Lord, Hallelujah," and his concept of praising in the Spirit and lengthy congregational responses was as disturbing to me as to anyone else.

Perhaps it was undue pride in our lovely new auditorium, so much more elegant than the "old barn" in which we had started, but this man seemed to lack the refinement and decorum to which we had grown accustomed. When we would introduce him as the speaker, instead of coming to the pulpit, he would put a chair alongside it, strap on his accordion, and begin to sing Scriptures set to music. Once we learned a verse, he would repeat it again and again. We were not used to this and grew very impatient with it.

Little by little, however, we began to learn that singing from the intellect is not the same as singing in the Spirit. He was teaching us how to move from a body function to a Spirit response. He would emphasize the truth of the words and then have us sing them again, until there was something within us reaching out in our song.

Another thing struck me: he never seemed to be in a hurry. I feared he had been in the southern hemisphere so long he had forgotten that Americans keep rather regular hours. After he felt we had initiated some response from within to the song we were singing, he took off his accordion, and we expected him to begin preaching. But he didn't. He insisted that all of us leave our padded pews and stand close together at the front of the auditorium.

Then he exhorted us to raise our hands and vocally express our love, praise, and adoration to the Lord. Few of us knew how. I could express myself emotionally on the organ, but not vocally. He often read a Psalm and emphasized that praise is a vocal expression. Then he urged us to try it again.

The patience and great faith of this man did eventually overcome our timidity, and suddenly we found ourselves, however weakly, expressing worship and praise! What's more, we looked around at one another, and if we felt more than a bit foolish, at least we were all in the same boat.

Morning and night, this brother exhorted, exemplified, and encouraged us in praise. He urged us to raise our hands unto the Lord. Now that was going a bit far! I've never seen such an instant plague of arthritis. Not only did our hands feel like they were lead weights, our arm muscles ached after only a few seconds. I think we could have done twenty push-ups easier than we could raise our hands unto the Lord for thirty seconds. What bondage had to be broken in our lives! Each of us felt that the entire congregation was gazing only at us. If we happened to touch another while raising our hands, we felt we had to apologize and start over. How God must have shook His head at us!

Finally, in one last do-or-die effort to break our fears and acute self-awareness, this dear man of God urged us to march around the building one night. And after that, he suggested dancing before the Lord! How glad I was that it was so late that no passersby might chance to look in on us. This was positively unreal! And, yet, unmistakedly, all of these were clear commands in the Bible, and I had to admit that every time we obeyed them, it seemed to bring us a little nearer the presence of God.

Nearer the presence of God … And then I remembered what He had promised that day on the roof. So this was how He was going to do it! I think from that moment all of my deepest resistance was broken, but it would be some time before I could embrace these new ways with anything approaching his enthusiasm. Toward the end of his stay, he brought a tape recording he had made in a church that knew how to relax in praising the Lord. He intended to play it for the evening service and was kind enough to give me a preview of it in private. Just listening to it proved embarrassing to me. How could they worship so uninhibitedly, so naturally, so honestly?

I couldn't give him any reason why I didn't want that tape played in our evening service, but he recognized and respected my fears. He did say that if I continued to lead my people in vocal worship, the day would come when we, too, would enter into just such unrestrained, open praise. I only smiled, for I no more believed that than Martha believed Lazarus would come out of his tomb.

As the week ended, we all had mixed emotions. Relief and regret. The pressure had been heavy, but we had come a long way in seven days. Most of us somehow regretted having the ministry end, for we had experienced something of God hitherto unknown to us—the warm glow that His presence produces, a flow of love that exceeded our former experiences, an operation of spiritual gifts that brought us communication from God. We certainly felt we had been "in heavenly places in Christ Jesus" (Ephesians 2:6).

And when our visitor left, we were glad that he had promised to return, although that schedule was many weeks in the future.

2

The Purpose of Praise

We worship and adore Thee ..." sang the sanctuary choir as an invitation to worship. The opening words were lost amidst muffled whispers from the congregation. The impact of the new choir robes was sensational, and I smiled at the "coincidence" of their arrival, the very Sunday after the second visit of the man of God. It was so much greater than the one two months before. We had gotten over the shock of having to praise vocally, and actually, it hadn't seemed too hard to praise last week. In fact, I rather enjoyed standing with my congregation in front of the pulpit and praising in whatever manner the visitor suggested. At times, it seemed he went too far, but I guess all teaching requires an over-emphasis of the subject to enforce the learning process.

"Bowing down before Thee ..."

I shifted my weight gently, to turn inconspicuously toward the soprano section and get a good look at the robes. Yes, gold was the right color. It blended perfectly with the new carpet and the birch pews.

Slowly turning back to face the congregation, I could see

that the pianist, organist, and the choir director were also resplendent in new robes. Now everything was in balance. I had nearly driven the men of the congregation crazy with my obsession for having this auditorium balanced. They had to re-do the steps to the platform twice because I had found them of slightly different heights.

"Songs of praises ringing ... " the choir continued.

The congregation was listening now, not just looking. I wondered just how much I should emphasize praise this morning. It would be different now that he had gone.

We had come a long way from the day when I had thrown my hatchet through the roof, and I didn't want to rock the boat too severely—especially right now. Having finished the building, we were starting mortgage payments now, and this was no time to create dissension.

"Hallelujahs ringing ... "

I didn't want to give them too much praise. But how much was too much? Life was full of praise. Manufacturers praised their product. Parents praised their children and were outdone only by the grandparents. Men praised their automobiles or their favorite football teams; women praised their hairdressers, their culinary prowess, or their wardrobes. Children praised, sportsmen praised, pastors praised, and even politicians liked to "point with pride."

Praise was certainly not foreign to our way of life; it was an integral part of it! It seemed to be ingrained in our basic human nature to spontaneously praise whatever we valued. Could we view a great masterpiece of art without giving an exclamation of praise? Could we listen to a symphony skillfully performed without loudly praising the conductor and the orchestra by clapping our hands? We even sent compliments to the chef after enjoying an unusually delicious meal. It was not so much that these things were "deserving" or "worthy," but that in order to fully savor our enjoyment, we had to give expression to our feelings. It completed us. It enhanced our delight. It seemed to seal the feeling of pleasure within us.

The choir director asked the congregation to stand and join the choir in a repeat of the chorus, "We worship and adore Thee … "

"Adore Thee …" Of course! If God was among the things we valued, it was normal to release our inner being in praise to Him and about Him. It was not so much that He needed to hear it as that we needed to say it and to hear ourselves saying it. The conductor of the symphony didn't "need" to hear our applause (although, obviously, he enjoyed and rightly deserved it) as much as we needed to release our inner feelings in an acceptable way.

Yesterday's crowd at the football stadium would have gone crazy if they hadn't been allowed to express themselves at our first win of the season. The team didn't need the praise in order to make the touchdown; they made it before the crowd began praising. It was the spectators who benefited from the clapping, yelling, and waving of hands, hats, and banners.

"You may be seated. Let's turn in our songbooks this morning to page … "

Songbooks! We didn't use them at all last week. He had us sing from the New Testament. It was an interesting experience to sing directly from God's Word. The very singing became praise, and we never stumbled searching for words. It was going to take a while to develop a praise vocabulary.

In his book *Reflections on the Psalms*, C.S. Lewis wrote, "I had not noticed how the humblest, and at the same time most balanced and capacious minds, praised most, while the cranks, misfits and malcontents, praised least. The good critics found something to praise in many imperfect works; the bad ones continually narrowed the list of books we might be allowed to read. The healthy and unaffected man, even if luxuriously brought up and widely experienced in good cookery, could praise a very modest meal; the dyspeptic and the snob found fault with all. Except where intolerably adverse circumstances interfere, praise almost seems to be inner health made audible."[1]

"Inner health made audible ... " Spiritual health made audible. Those who had spiritual health found praise to be quite natural to their inner nature, although, with many of us, it had been repressed by religious training. But praise was there! It was an expression of inner strength to praise, and it was an exercising of that strength when praise was expressed. I remembered, as a boy, attending camp meetings where Dr. Charles Price was the speaker. Praise was often the keynote in his services. I had seen congregations rise to their feet during his sermon and spontaneously praise for up to an hour while he joined us in worship, then concluded his sermon when we were seated again. It was as though they could not help themselves, something within so cried out to be expressed.

And there was an invitation to it, a spontaneous appeal for others to join in. And after all, that's what "Hallelujah" really meant: "Praise ye the Lord." It was much like asking, "Wasn't that delicious? Isn't that beautiful?" We want to share our enjoyment, for life unshared is life half-lived.

Yet it wasn't simply inner health that caused us to praise at a concert or ball game. Without that health, we might be unable to praise, but the motivation was an outer stimulus. It seemed that the emotional response was in direct proportion to the emotional stimuli. The greater the excitement, the greater the shouting. I wondered if we'd ever get so excited over Jesus, and what He had done for us, that we'd just have to release the pressure of excitement in shouts of praise. This was why our guest spent so much time talking about Jesus and what He had provided for us: it stimulated us to excitement and anticipation, and we somewhat spontaneously rejoiced!

The more he had talked about the Lord, the warmer my heart had felt toward Jesus. My love had grown greatly this past week. And, come to think of it, this, too, had motivated me to praise.

Just as one of the keys to successful courtship was communication, and the act of communicating love not only expressed it but completed it, so one of the keys to a more intimate relationship with the Lord Jesus Christ was love communicated. It amplified the love within us, it enhanced our enjoyment of Him, it enlarged our capacity for Him and made our existence more meaningful. The Scottish catechism said that man's chief end was "to glorify God and enjoy Him forever." Fully to enjoy was to glorify. In commanding us to glorify Him, God was inviting us to enjoy Him. And in enjoying Him, we would, because of our very nature, invite others to enjoy Him with us.

"Let's stand together and sing this chorus once more before Pastor Cornwall comes to lead us in praise and worship."

I wondered if I could do it. It seemed so easy the way he did it. But I must keep it balanced. But balanced to what? To their inner spiritual health that demands expression? To the stimulus of God's presence? Balanced with their love responses to God? To God's commands to praise? Yet we've been spiritually healthy without praise. We've been greatly stimulated by God and His Word. We have shown our love for God by many selfless deeds without praising. Why didn't we praise then? And why did we have the beginning desire to praise now?

C.S. Lewis said, "I had never noticed that all enjoyment spontaneously overflows into praise, unless (sometimes even if) shyness or the fear of boring others is deliberately brought in to check it."[2]

Shyness, fear...checking it? Of course, that was the trouble: our reluctance to overcome this "shyness"—a polite term for self-centeredness.

At the close of the song, I said a fast prayer, stepped into the pulpit, and said, "Let's lift our hands unto the Lord and praise His name."

I realized that I was on display. I was not standing with my people, I was facing them. A few people began to lift their hands, and some braver souls were already gently expressing vocal praise, but I was paralyzed. My arms didn't want to move. I felt a flash of terror, knowing that the congregation in front of me and the choir behind me were all watching to see how I would lead them in praise. All sense of spirituality had drained out of me, leaving me with a familiar back problem: a broad yellow stripe which extended from the base of my skull to where my spine met my pelvis. Jesus, help me! By sheer force of will, I got my hands lifted to the pulpit level and managed to express a few praise-the-Lords. Nervous coughs and shuffling revealed that I was not alone in my self-consciousness. We wanted to praise, but it was hardly "flowing like a river."

This was the crucial moment. Under the faith and guidance of another, we had entered into some enjoyment of praise. Could we maintain it and grow in it on our own? If I couldn't break through my self-consciousness today, right now, no matter what it might cost me, I was convinced we would plunge back to where we had started from, worse off, because we had had a taste and knew the promise.

"Look," I said, "let's all gather together at the front of the auditorium. Choir, come off the platform and join the congregation. God's Word declares in Psalm 100, verse 4, 'Enter into His gates with thanksgiving, and into His courts with praise.' " As they came forward, I went on to explain, "In the tabernacle in the wilderness, God's place of habitation was the Holy of Holies. It sat in a courtyard surrounded by a linen fence which had only one gate. Anyone approaching God came through that gate and walked through the courtyard to get to the tabernacle in which God dwelt. The gate is called "thanksgiving" and the court is called "praise." That is why

Psalm 22:3 declares that God inhabits the praises of His people. The place of His dwelling is in the midst of the courtyard of praise. If we desire to approach God, we must come through praise. If we would enter petitions before God, we must also come through thanksgiving, as Philippians 4:6 tells us: 'With thanksgiving let your requests be made known unto God.'

"All right," I said, looking around at all of us sheepishly gathered up front, "now that we're united physically, let's get united in the activity of praise. So no one will feel he is being looked at, let's all close our eyes and focus our attention on our lovely Lord Jesus. Now, even if it takes all the willpower you've got, lift your hands and faces Godward and tell Him that you love Him."

I strapped on the roving microphone to free me from the pulpit, lifted my hands, and joined my congregation in telling God that I loved Him. Slowly I moved from one end of the platform to the other, praying and praising with more than a little desperation.

Finally, when in my heart I had utterly given up, the log-jam began to move. Almost imperceptibly, the volume of praise began to increase.

A pair of half-raised arms reached to a full stretch. A bowed head became a lifted head. Whispered words became exclamations of praise. Some wept, some shouted, some sang softly, and a few gently clapped their hands. Bit by bit, we seemed to be tuning one another out and tuning God in.

It was obvious, from facial expressions and the changing level and pitch of the vocal praise, that as some broke through to victory, others were coming under the dealings of God. What had started as a simple praise session had, for some, become a time of direct confrontation.

Our reactions to this manifestation of the presence of God were as varied as our individual personalities. But by this point, our reactions no longer mattered. We felt like Mary, who had sat at the feet of Jesus, or like Lazarus, who had just come forth from the tomb at the call of the Lord.

As the level of praise subsided, I led them in a chorus of praise that sparked them to a renewed outpouring of worship to God. Gently, but very pronouncedly, we became conscious of a sense of the divine presence of God greater than we had ever known before. It was as though we had bridged the gap between His world and ours, and we were on the outskirts of His glorious realm.

An overwhelming peace filled the auditorium, and there was an inner experience of alternating love and joy—like ocean waves, one after another, cascading onto the beach. It seemed the light of God's countenance had pierced to the very depth of our souls, not only revealing hidden things, but bringing life and healing to the inner man.

My wife, seated at the piano ready to assist me with any worship chorus I might signal, was allowed to see angels of the Lord walking in our midst.

The crisis was over. We had survived a strong emphasis on praise without the high faith level of our visiting minister. We were on our way to becoming a praising church.

During the year that followed, I preached on praise almost exclusively. Having been shown that the path into the presence of God was praise, I wanted to learn about individual praise, collective praise, praise from our spirit, praise in the Holy Spirit, praise in song, praise with the Word, and so on. And I not only preached praise, I continued to have the people gather at the front to practice it.

Needless to say, all this was not done without some repercussions. Some of our people decided it was time to change churches, and they did. Others felt it was time to change pastors. But I remained convinced it was time, instead, to hold fast to our new approach to God.

It was not long until our new form of worship was known throughout the community and then in our denominational circles. We received little encouragement and lots of criticism, but we really didn't care: we were finding a freedom and fellowship with God we had not experienced before, and we had no desire to return to our former arid and sterile ways.

We were excited—and a little awed—with what God was doing. Our praise was producing the realized presence of God, moving us beyond the rituals of worship into a vital, personal confrontation with Him. It was lifting us out of a self- and need-centeredness, to a Christ-centeredness. And now that we seemed to have the handles, we were not about to let go.

There were other unexpected benefits of praise. It brought a new honesty into our midst. It helped us enlarge our concepts of God. In teaching us how to release our emotions of love and joy, it began to have a noticeable effect in our church's marriages and interpersonal relationships. It moved us from negative to positive attitudes. It changed our services from identification to participation. It began to mold our congregation into a family unit, for once we learned to flow love to God, we began to learn how to love one another.

Again and again, in the weeks that followed, God told us, through a prophetic word, that our praising delighted Him, that He enjoyed it, that it brought us into a warm relationship with Him that was very satisfying to Him. One particularly forceful word of prophecy was given in which the Lord declared that our worship and praise had brought great pleasure to Him.

Pleasure to God? That was a new thought. Somehow I had thought only of God bringing pleasure to us. Yet one of the last five praise psalms declares, "For the Lord taketh pleasure in his people" (Psalm 149:4). And the Psalmist cries, "Bless the Lord, O my soul" (Psalm 104:1), not "Bless my soul, O Lord." We, the lesser, are invited (commanded) to bless, honor, magnify, extol, give pleasure to the greater.

Two New Testament books seem to reflect this truth. In Revelation 4:11 we read, "Thou art worthy, O Lord, to receive glory and honour and power: for thou hast created all things, and for thy pleasure they are and were created."

Ephesians 1:12 states, "that we should be to the praise of his glory." The Twentieth Century New Testament translates it, "that we should enhance His glory." As surely as God made woman to enhance the man, God made man to enhance His God. As woman became an extension of the man (Ephesians 5:28 commands "men to love their wives as their own bodies"), so man became somewhat of an extension of God. It was the breath, or Spirit, of God that put life in the first man. That man was said to have been created in "the image of God." God told Adam that to be completed, he must be joined to his wife. The two of them made one. She completed him, and he her.

Just so, man completes God, and God completes man. Not in the sense that God is incomplete as a person without the man, but that His sense of satisfaction is not complete without man. God desires and yearns for a close relationship with man.

When a small daughter crawls up on her father's lap, hugs him, and kisses him, does this make him a complete man? No. Does he have to have this? No. Does he desire and enjoy it? Oh, yes! This completes his enjoyment of fatherhood. Just so, my expressed love and adoration for God completes His enjoyment of being our Father. God loves me as an extension of Himself, and delights and receives genuine pleasure when I respond to that love in expressions of praise and worship.

One morning, as I sent the congregation back to their seats to prepare to worship the Lord in giving, I reflected on the fact that it always seemed to be during the praise time that God had communicated with us. I remembered the 29th Psalm which begins, "Give unto the Lord ... the glory due unto his name; worship the Lord in the beauty of holiness," and then continues, in verses 3-5, 7-9, speaking of "the voice of the Lord." I also remembered Psalm 68:32-33 saying, "Sing unto God ... O sing praises unto the Lord; ... lo, he doth send out his voice, and that a mighty voice." As we enter into His presence in praise, we open a channel of communication that gives God an opportunity to speak to us and to be heard.

I remember when I was taking flying lessons that I was very nervous the first time my instructor had me fly out of a radio-controlled field. I had practiced the procedures repeatedly, but this was "for real." I picked up the microphone, pushed in the button on the side, and said, "Eugene tower, this is 5723W, ready for take-off." Total silence. I repeated my message, but still no answer. After what seemed a very long period of time, I made my call again. This time the instructor noticed that I had not released the mike button. In my fright, I had frozen "on" the switch which made it possible for me to speak, but cut off all reception. As I released the button, I heard the tower saying, "Seven, eight, nine, zero ... how do you read me, 23W?"

They had been speaking all the time! I had just blocked out all reception pressing down on the "talk button" on the microphone.

Too often, prayer causes us to hold the switch on the communications, blocking off reception from God. When we praise, we give Him a chance to speak to us.

Proverbs 27:21 says, "As the fining pot for silver, and the furnace for gold; so is a man to praise."

So often it is during praise time, when we have heated our spirits in worship and have the touch of the presence of God around us, that sublimated thoughts, desires, and attitudes rise to the surface. We may have thought we had dealt with these things, but we had only stuffed them down into our subconscious. As we are broken and heated in His presence, these things are separated from the precious metal of our spirits, and rise to the surface. Only then are we able to get them to His Cross, to be cleansed from them by His mighty power, to be freed from them by the action of the Divine Smelter's nail-scarred hand, skimming them from our surface.

When asked how he knew the silver was sufficiently pure to be poured into the molds, an old-time refiner said, "I know it is ready when I am able to see my face mirrored undistorted in the molten metal." Will our Divine Smelter give up on us before He has removed the impurities that distort His image in our lives? Will He not encourage us to heat and reheat our lives again and again until all the inner impurities have been released and submitted to His hand? Praise is the pot and the furnace that gives God a chance to further purify our lives. The greater the heat, the greater the release.

How often, during praise sessions, have I seen individuals go to one another to make things right. Fathers straightened things out with children, wives with husbands, and vice versa. Many were saved just standing during a praise session. More people were filled with the Holy Spirit while we were in praise than when we laid hands on them. And the healings that took place—outstanding is the only word for them!

During the week, tradesmen would remark that they could "feel a presence" even in the empty building. God was, indeed, keeping His pledge to show me a safe way into His divine presence!

End Notes

1 C.S. Lewis, Reflections on the Psalms (London: Collins Fontana Books) p. 19.

2 Ibid., p.23.

3

The Pattern of Praise

At the time our congregation began to enter into praise, we already had members from at least twenty denominational backgrounds, worshiping together. Although they were, for the most part, Spirit-filled, they did not classify themselves as Pentecostals nor did they consider themselves members of the denomination whose name was on the church building. In fact, each seemed to retain an inner identification with the denomination in which he had worshiped for so many years. Although we never used the title, I suppose we could have been classified as a community church.

With such diversity of backgrounds, not surprisingly, there was an equal diversity of concepts of praise. Our members from a liturgical background saw praise quite differently from the classic Pentecostals in our midst, and though we all agreed that praise was proper, we found ourselves divided on a proper way of expressing that praise.

Realizing that up to this point we had simply copied the method of praising that had been brought to us, we set ourselves to search the Scriptures to see if God had revealed a pattern of praise. It seemed far better to go directly to the original pattern than to copy something that has been "adapted" from it.

I remember violating this principle once as a young pastor. We were constructing a new church in Kennewick, Washington, and doing it entirely by volunteer labor. When it was time to raise the rafters, we borrowed a large radial saw to cut them to size and shape. The chief carpenter in our church drew a pattern on the first 2 x 10 piece of timber and cut it to shape. He told me to use this as the pattern for all succeeding cuts. Most of our work was done at night, and I had volunteered to spend my days that week pre-cutting the rafters so that when we had a crew of men, they could raise the rafters into place.

It soon became obvious to me that using the pattern meant the handling of that twenty-four-foot piece of heavy lumber repeatedly, whereas the board I had just cut was already in position to act as a pattern for the new board. All I had to do was draw a line at the end with a pencil and cut it.

I was rather proud of my shortcut and happily showed the large stack of pre-cut rafters to the builder when work-night arrived. He properly congratulated me for my work and began supervising the raising of the rafters.

It was not long, however, before it was obvious that something was wrong. There was an inconsistency in the length of the rafters. Each board was longer than the preceding one by the thickness of a pencil mark because I had not continued to use the original pattern. Such a minute variation had not seemed worth considering at the time—but it was multiplied one hundred times (the number of rafters I had cut).

The rafters were useless. The work-night was lost, the days of labor were wasted, and ninety-nine rafters had to be re-cut (the first one, made from the original pattern, was usable).

Would it not be equally foolish to pattern our praise solely on the behavior pattern of men who learned it from other men who learned it from others, and so on, back to those who may have originally learned it from the Scripture? Why not seek out the divine pattern at the beginning?

So, continuing our search for a Divine pattern, we rediscovered two books of the Bible that give us glimpses into the heavens—in the Old Testament, Isaiah, and in the New, Revelation. While other writers of the Bible had visions of the living creatures of Heaven (notably Ezekiel), it is Isaiah and John, living hundreds of years apart, from diverse cultures and different physical circumstances (Isaiah, tutor of kings; John, prisoner of kings), speaking separate languages, who see and similarly report the magnificence of heavenly praise.

Isaiah's account is given in chapter six. The first four verses tell us, "In the year that king Uzziah died I saw also the Lord sitting upon a throne, high and lifted up, and his train filled the temple. Above it stood the seraphims: each one had six wings; with twain he covered his face, and with twain he covered his feet, and with twain he did fly. And one cried unto another, and said, Holy, holy, holy, is the Lord of hosts: the whole earth is full of his glory. And the posts of the door moved at the voice of him that cried, and the house was filled with smoke."

The seraphim described here are very high-ranking beings of the angelic order. Many feel they are the highest of God's angelic hosts, while others feel the cherubim described by Ezekiel are the first rank of God's heavenly order (Ezekiel 1). Isaiah records that at the time of his visit to the temple, these great creatures of God's service were exchanging praises unto the Lord upon the throne in a sort of antiphonal chant or cry. So great was the volume of their praise that the "posts of the door" moved (v. 4).

We also read that the house filled with the smoke or incense of worship. Little wonder, then, that the Psalmist often speaks of a loud shout being germane to praise, or that the New Testament writers tell us that the Lord's return will be "with a shout" (1 Thessalonians 4:16).

From the shout of Israel at Jericho (Joshua 6:20), to the shouts at the laying of the foundation of the Temple (Ezra 3:11-13), through the exhortations of the Psalmists and prophets, shouting, as part of worship, is mentioned often in the Bible. Very rarely (Habakkuk 2:20) are we told to "keep silence before him," while many times we are enjoined to shout: "Clap your hands, all ye people; shout unto God with the voice of triumph" (Psalm 47:1); "Let all those that put their trust in thee rejoice: let them ever shout for joy" (Psalm 5:11).

It is not that God desires the volume or puts a premium on noise, but that man needs the release of his pent-up joyful emotions that shouting can bring him.

Think of our earlier analogy. Just let your favorite football team unexpectedly intercept a pass and run it all the way back for a touchdown, and the stimulated emotions rise to such a high peak that they are released in a loud shout, often accompanied with emphatic physical gestures. The same emotional rise occurs when saints actually see the Lord seated on His throne; the work is accomplished, the victory is won, nothing remains to be done. It is not amiss or improper to express those infused emotions in an electrifying shout of praise, when this is an honest expression of inner feelings.

True, not everyone shouts at football games and not everyone shouts in a worship service, but I have sometimes wondered if the non-shouters really understood what was going on down on the field. Can we see Christ as the complete conqueror of all our enemies and not at least "feel" a shout rising within us? It is obvious, from Isaiah's vision, that the angelic hosts cannot! Just the sight of the Conqueror at rest evoked loud praises unto His name!

When we turned to the Book of Revelation, we saw varied forms of worship transpiring. The four living creatures (RSV) cry, "Holy, holy, holy, Lord God Almighty, which was, and is, and is to come" (4:8). They are giving "glory and honor and thanks" to the Lord (4:9). The twenty-four elders prostrate themselves "and worship him that liveth for ever and ever, and cast their crowns before the throne, saying, Thou art worthy, O Lord, to receive glory and honour and power: for thou hast created all things, and for thy pleasure they are and were created" (4:10).

All, except the casting of the crowns and prostrate bowing, is vocal, audible expression from living, rational beings unto the Lord. In chapter five, a great multitude of angels joins the living creatures (RSV) and elders of chapter four. John tries to describe their number by saying, "The number of them was ten thousand times ten thousand, and thousands of thousands" (Revelation 5:11) which, if we dared to take it literally, would be in excess of one hundred million angels, all praising with a "loud voice" (Revelation 5:12).

In verse thirteen we read, "And every creature which is in heaven, and on the earth, and under the earth, and such as are in the sea, and all that are in them, heard I saying, Blessing, and honour, and glory, and power, be unto him that sitteth upon the throne, and unto the Lamb for ever and ever." This is in complete harmony with Psalm 148 which also calls upon all the creation and created beings to unite in praising God. The day is coming when everyone shall praise the Lord vocally and unitedly.

In Revelation 7:9-10, we read, "After this I beheld, and, lo, a great multitude, which no man could number, of all nations, and kindreds, and people, and tongues, stood before the throne, and before the Lamb, clothed with white robes, and palms in their hands; And cried with a loud voice, saying, Salvation to our God which sitteth upon the throne, and unto the Lamb." In the next two verses, all the angels, and elders, and living creatures (RSV) in heaven join in this vociferous expression of praise, saying, "Amen: Blessing, and glory, and wisdom, and thanksgiving, and honour, and power, and might, be unto our

God for ever and ever. Amen" (Revelation 7:12).

In January of 1973, while I was ministering on this theme in the downtown Presbyterian Church in Bogota, Colombia, the pastor told me that my sermon had given him increased motivation to want to go to Heaven: he wanted to see twenty-four elders who would consistently fall down before the presence of the Lord and worship. Every mention of the Elders in the Book of Revelation shows them worshiping.

A group in Heaven express their praise in song: "And they sing the song of Moses the servant of God, and the song of the Lamb, saying, Great and marvellous are thy works, Lord God Almighty; just and true are thy ways, thou King of saints. Who shall not fear thee, O Lord, and glorify thy name? for thou only art holy: for all nations shall come and worship before thee; for thy judgments are made manifest" (Revelation 15:3-4).

Both the Song of Moses and the Song of the Lamb are songs of deliverance. Both declare that the work is already done. They are not songs of faith looking forward to deliverance, but songs of fact, looking back at deliverance. This group is motivated to praise by remembering Christ's finished work.

In chapter nineteen, we again see mass worship and praise with shoutings, adulations, prostration, and declarations of the greatness of God. So overwhelming was the laudation, that John seemed to be at a loss for descriptive terms. He writes, "And I heard as it were the voice of a great multitude, and as the voice of many waters, and as the voice of mighty thunderings, saying, Alleluia: for the Lord God omnipotent reigneth" (Revelation 19:6). A colosseum of shouting people—a cascading waterfall of praises—a thundering of praise!

From these visions into the heavenlies, then, we got a beginning pattern of the nature and performance of praise. It is vocal, often voluminous. It is sometimes antiphonal, sometimes united, sometimes singular. Often it is sung, even more often it is shouted. Not infrequently it is accompanied by standing, raising the hands, bowing, prostrating, casting of crowns before Him, etc.

We did not see these things as demands of the Scriptures, nor as exhortations similar to those in the Psalms, but what holy men of old actually witnessed taking place in Heaven—not merely what should be done, what was being done. This is the divine pattern, the exemplar, the protocol of praise! Anything less than this may be fine, but must accept the tag, "Made according to man's pattern."

During our search for a pattern of praise, we also noted the many instances where angels were commissioned to communicate with man. Their communication usually included praise to God. The best-known example is the appearance of the angelic host to the shepherds on Bethlehem's hillsides to announce the birth of Jesus: "And suddenly there was with the angel a multitude of the heavenly host praising God, and saying, Glory to God in the highest, and on earth peace, good will toward men. … And the shepherds returned, glorifying and praising God for all the things that they had heard and seen, as it was told unto them" (Luke 2:13-14, 20).

Because there are so many different terms used in Scripture for adulation and praise unto God, we sometimes miss seeing the full role it plays in the Word. These glimpses into heavenly praising helped our congregation see that all praise is worship. We sometimes called it the "vocal end" of worship. It is even one aspect of prayer, a portion of thanksgiving, a releasing of joy, the "lesser" blessing the "greater."

We soon assembled twenty or more similes or analogies for praise. Some refer to various ways of expressing praise vocally. Some point to the use of the hands in praise, while others direct attention to the posture of the body in praise. (The serious student of praise will find a listing of methods of praise in the appendix.)

During the year that I preached almost exclusively on praise, I decided to see how widely praise is taught throughout the Bible. In re-reading the Bible that year, I kept an orange felt pen handy and underscored verses that mentioned praise. I was continually astonished at the frequency of mention, although this was exactly what I was searching for.

It became excitingly clear to us that praise was hardly confined to the book of the Psalms and that praise did not originate with man; it began with God. Well-meaning religious men have not commanded us to praise, God has!

If praise had had its origins in man, we would have had both the right and the responsibility to criticize it, revise it, to question it, or even completely disregard it as not being germane for the twentieth century.

But since praise had its origins in God's Heaven, we felt we had to accept and participate in it. We observed, that there had developed such a discrepancy between the original pattern of praise and worship and the present product called "worship" as to challenge the credulity of the most naive among us. We had been using each latest cut as our pattern for the next rafter. Now we felt it was time to get back to the original, divine pattern, and "do our first works over."

4

The Paradigms of Praise

In the early 1950s at the church I was pastoring in Kennewick, Washington, we were bursting at the seams and had to build. But how and what? We had as many ideas as we had people. It seemed everyone wanted to build a church just like the one back home. In a denominational paper I saw a picture of a church that interested me. I wrote to the pastor on the East Coast, and asked if I could borrow a set of plans to study. The sketches and elevation drawings that he sent completely satisfied both me and my board that this was the type of structure we needed. It would nicely fit our property, it was so simple to construct that the men of the congregation could do most of the work, yet it was of an architectural style that blended well with the homes in the area.

We posted the architect's drawings on the bulletin board, expecting the congregation's instant approval. Instead, we found them confused, unable to visualize the proposed structure from the drawings. They could not transform a drawing into three-dimensional thought. Although we had what we thought was the perfect pattern for our building, people only became bewildered.

After two weeks of increasing confusion, I decided to do something about it. I would make a scale model. It involved many hours of work, but when it was accurate in every detail, including lighting, I put the model on display in the front of the church in place of the sketches. The reaction was most gratifying. When they could see a model of what the architect had in mind, members of the congregation were thrilled. That week, at a business meeting, they voted unanimously to build "according to the model." We broke ground within a week.

In the same way, God's patterns are often difficult for us to translate into action because of our inability to properly visualize or comprehend spiritual things. Since we are so dependent upon our senses, and our acquisition of knowledge demands a proceeding from the known to the unknown, God has often given us paradigms—models—on Earth that represent the reality of the heavens.

The Old Testament abounds with models, types, symbols, or paradigms of the reality that was to be revealed later. Who has not thrilled at the abundant (over 100) types of Christ to be seen in the life of Joseph; or at the pattern of faith seen in Abraham; or the pattern of redemption seen in the paschal lamb? These gave us a foretaste, a prefiguring, a perception of that which was yet to come. They presented us with keys of understanding that we might recognize the real when it arrived, as surely as my sending a photograph of myself to a pastor before arrival in his city makes it easy for him to identify me as I step off the airplane.

While there are, unquestionably, many more paradigms of praise than I have yet discovered in the Bible, there are three major models that richly illustrate praise.

Judah, a Paradigm of Praise

The very first use of the word "praise" in the Scriptures is in Genesis 29:35 in connection with the birth of Judah whose name means "praise."

There was a serious conflict between Leah and Rachel, the two wives of Jacob. Leah, who was forced upon Jacob in a most deceitful switch at the wedding (Jacob had labored seven years for Rachel), had, as her only claim to her husband's affections, borne him three sons: Reuben, Simeon, and Levi. It was at the birth of the third son that she felt that she and Jacob were really "joined" (Genesis 29:34). Up to this time, there had been a legal and physical joining, but now, she felt, there would be a joining in the spiritual union of the marriage. Following this "joining," this coming into a true, spiritual relationship one with the other, she conceived again and bore a son. It is in this circumstance that Scripture declares, "Now will I praise the Lord: therefore she called his name Judah [Praise] " (Genesis 29:35).

How fitting an introduction to the ministry of praise, for it is not being "legally" related to the Lord that brings forth praise but the "spiritual" union that brings us into a relationship—spirit, soul, and body—with Him.

The son that was the outgrowth of a complete union was himself to be the father of a family, a tribe, and a nation—all bearing his name of Praise. From this man was to come the great King David, and the greater than David, the Lord Jesus Christ himself! Keep in mind that Judah always means praise, no matter where you find it in the Bible.

Let's look at a few key references to Judah in the four major divisions of the Old Testament.

Judah in the Pentateuch

In the Pentateuch, the first five books of the Bible, the name Judah appears more than forty times.

The historical portions of these books of the law do not reveal Judah as being perfect nor his ways totally pleasing unto God. Yet when the dying Jacob called his sons to his death-bed and spoke prophetically to each of them, his words to Judah were, "Judah is a lion's whelp: from the prey, my son, thou art gone up: he stooped down, he couched as a lion, and as an old lion; who shall rouse him up? The sceptre shall not depart from Judah, nor a lawgiver from between his feet, until Shiloh come; and unto him shall the gathering of the people be" (Genesis 49:9-10).

I am not aware of any disagreement among scholars as to the basic meaning of this prophecy, a clear prognostication of the coming of the Lord Jesus Christ. In his complete concordance to the Bible, James Strong says of the word Shiloh, that it is "an epithet of the Messiah." Of Jesus it is said, "The Lion of the tribe of Judah, the Root of David, hath prevailed to open the book, and to loose the seven seals thereof" (Revelation 5:5).

Whether he was Lion or Lawgiver, the promise was that Shiloh, the Messiah, the Christ, would come out of Judah, Praise. Does not our deliverance, our defense, our directive consistently come out of praise? Non-praisers often live in terror of the adversary who "as a roaring lion, walketh about, seeking whom he may devour" (I Pet. 5:8) while the true praisers live in trust that the Lion of the tribe of Judah shall prevail over every onslaught of the devil. Psalm 81 teaches us that if we will praise God, "There shall no strange god be in thee" (81:9). Praise is our greatest defense against the eruption of demonic activity in our generation.

Another graphic illustration of praise is the order in which God had Israel set up camp in the wilderness. According to Numbers 2:2-3, the camp of Judah was placed on the east side, facing both the rising sun and the only entrance into the tabernacle enclosure.

It is always the praiser who gets the first glimpse of the rising of the "Sun of Righteousness" (Malachi 4:2) over the horizon, because the man who praises has set his face expecting the rising sun to pierce the darkness. Others will see the light later. He will see the advanced rays of the sunrise!

It was the standard of Judah, bearing the symbol of the lion, which was pitched directly east of the tabernacle. Only the priesthood itself had readier access to the place of worship than the tribe of Judah. While everyone in the camp had access to the tabernacle and its outer court of worship, many of them had quite a journey to get there. The praisers, Judah, dwelt next-door to the gate! I do not doubt that there are non-praisers who gain access to the presence of the Lord, but their route is often long, arduous, and wearisome, and when they finally arrive, they find they must enter in through praise, for that is the name of the court.

Deuteronomy 33:7 records a fourfold blessing of "praise" (Judah). Moses was prophetically blessing each of the twelve tribes of Israel, and to Judah he said, "Hear, Lord, the voice of Judah, and bring him unto his people: let his hands be sufficient for him; and be thou an help to him from his enemies." This, too, is a working model of praise. Note first that Moses asked God to hear the voice of Judah, Praise. Praise will pierce through any hindering force and gain an audience with God.

Secondly, Moses pled that "praise" should unite the family ("bring him unto his people"). How moving it is to see how God is using praise to bring His body of believers together in this day and age. Praise is a magnet that draws believers of differing concepts and backgrounds together, uniting them in worship, fellowship, and family.

Observe, also, that praise was to have strength equal to the task ("Let his hands be sufficient for him"). How appropriate that the Psalmist couples praises to the Lord with strength, "shewing to the generation to come the praises of the Lord, and his strength" (Psalm 78:4). The secret of strength for the

Christian is a praising heart! Well does the Word declare, "The joy of the Lord is your strength" (Nehemiah 8:10).

The fourth promise in this blessing of Judah is contained in, "Be thou an help to him from his enemies." Never lose sight of the truth that the praiser has access to deivine protection that the non-praising Christian does not have. The pledge of help was given to Judah, Praise.

Judah in the Historical Books

In the books of the law, we saw Judah prophetically. In the books of history, we see Judah performing. In Joshua fourteen we read of Caleb, the man chosen from the tribe of Judah to be one of the twelve spies sent to reconnoiter the land beyond Jordan. He, with Joshua, brought back a report of faith, and although the report was rejected, Caleb was allowed of God to live through the forty years of wandering during which the unbelieving Israelites died and were buried in the sands of the desert. In chapter fourteen, Caleb is reminding Joshua how the two of them had stood against the other ten spies in delivering the minority report. He declares, "I wholly followed the Lord my God" (Joshua 14:8); "the Lord hath kept me alive" (v. 10); "As yet I am as strong this day as I was in the day that Moses sent me" (v. 11); and "Now therefore give me this mountain" (v. 12).

A man who was of the tribe of Praise was preserved from disobedience, destruction, dissipation, and disinheritance. He took, as his inheritance, the very land that had been the possession of the giants that so terrified the children of Israel. Thank God for this small model of praise which reveals some of what praising can do for the practitioner.

The four areas of success reported by this man of Praise are often the main objectives of our Christian endeavors. Success in these areas comes to the man of the tribe of Praise.

In Judges 1:1-2 we read, "Now after the death of Joshua it came to pass, that the children of Israel asked the Lord, saying, Who shall go up for us against the Canaanites first, to fight against them? And the Lord said, Judah shall go up: behold, I have delivered the land into his hand." Praise shall enter the battle first! And God has already delivered the territory into the hand of Praise.

How literally this was proved in the case of Jehoshaphat, king of Judah, when he was secretly invaded by Moab and Ammon (2 Chronicles 20). God's instructions to him, given through a prophet, were to "stand ... still, and see the salvation of the Lord" (v. 17). Jehosphaphat worshiped the Lord, and then sent singers ahead of the army singing praises to the Lord (v. 21). Imagine sending the choir and orchestra ahead of the warriors! Yet it worked, for God moved in the camp and set the enemy against himself in an act of self-destruction. The army of Judah never drew a sword, but did spend three days collecting the spoil and loot from the dead bodies.

Saints who would learn to do battle for the Lord should first learn how to praise, for God sends praise as the shock troops to drive the enemy back before the rest of the army is allowed to join the battle.

In the beginning stages of our building program in Eugene, Oregon, I had a chance to personally try this use of praise. Stage one of the program required removal of the roof on the existing church, raising the walls to match the height of the joining structure. No sooner had we completed tearing off the old roof, than the sheriff served us with a cease-and-desist order which carried a penalty of $400 per day for continued construction. We had a legal building permit and had met all county requirements, as far as we knew. I immediately phoned the building department of our county government and was informed that our new building violated setback requirements of the zoning ordinance. I admitted knowledge of this but told them that the planning commission had granted us a waiver of this provision well over a year previously. The official with whom I was speaking was unaware of this variance grant and could not find it in his files. I offered him my copy but he would not accept it. He said his secretary was on vacation and we would have to wait her return to find the official copy in his files.

Anyone who has lived in Oregon knows it is apt to rain at any time of the year. Our entire church was exposed to rain damage. We had all materials on hand and had scheduled sufficient work parties to have the new roof completed within a week. Delay meant almost certain damage amounting to hundreds of dollars. Continued construction would open us to fines and penalties.

I reported the impasse to my work crew and asked them to join me in prayer. Then I instructed the men to continue working while I went to the prayer room. There I laid the official document on the bench and asked the Lord to read it. Then I began to praise Him for breaking through this hindrance. I paced back and forth in that room with my hands raised, doing nothing but praising God for stopping this hindrance to our building program.

In about an hour, the phone rang. It was the head of the county planning commission phoning to apologize for the inconvenience. The document in question had been found, and the mistake was obviously theirs. I asked to have permission to resume construction given in written form as protection against the legal paper that had been served. In less than an hour the sheriff drove up with the written apology. What could have been a month-long hassle with county officials was cleared up in less than two hours simply by praising the Lord. "Judah [Praise] shall go up [first]."

In 2 Samuel 2 we read that following the death of Saul in battle, it was the men of Praise, who "anointed David king over the house of Judah (v. 4). It is usually the men of praise who first enthrone Christ as Lord of all! Verses 8-9 tell us that Abner choose Ish-bosheth and anointed him king "over all Israel." Yet Judah recognized that the Lord had anointed David to be king, and they stood by God's choice. "The house of Judah followed David" (v. 10). It was seven-and-one-half years before David was received as king by anyone else. During those years, Judah had the joy of the divinely appointed leader and ingratiated themselves with him. Praisers are usually among the "firsts."

Praise produces proclaimers. We see this beautifully illustrated in 1 Kings 13:1: "And, behold, there came a man of God out of Judah by the word of the Lord unto Bethel." There are many workers for God and many ministers of the gospel, but usually the worker, or minister, who is called out specifically to be a "man of God" comes out of Judah, Praise. God seems to choose worshipers, praisers, men who understand the divine presence and are comfortable in it. What a shame that so few of our seminaries and Bible colleges offer courses in praise.

First Chronicles 12:23-40 lists the men who came to David to help him in his battle against the kingdom of Saul. The first group listed are "the children of Judah that bare shield and spear." These praisers knew how to use the shield of faith as well as the two-edged sword. They were men of combat. Of the groups listed, only Judahites and Naphtalites are said to be bearers of shield and spear. The praiser is as apt in defense as in offense! He can push the enemy back without exposing himself to the "fiery darts."

Judah in the Poetic Books

While the poetic books deal with praise very directly, the Psalms speak also of Judah as a paradigm of praise. "Let the daughters of Judah be glad" (48:11). "The daughters of Judah rejoiced" (97:8). The praisers and their children know joy and gladness, for they are dealing with the God of promises even more than with the promises of God. The Psalms say, "For God

41

... will build the cities of Judah: that they may dwell there, and have it in possession" (69:35), and "Judah was his sanctuary" (114:2). People who praise will have a place of habitation and thereby will give God a sanctuary in which to dwell: "But thou art holy, O thou that inhabitest the praises" (Psalm 22:3).

Judah in the Prophetic Books

Judah is mentioned more than 290 times in the prophetic books! Hosea 10:11 says, "Judah shall plow." How foolish to plant seed in unprepared soil that has become rock hard either from idleness or the many trampling feet of life's behavior patterns. The prophet suggests that praise can well plow the soil prior to the planting of the seed. As a pastor of a praising congregation for some years now, I can certainly attest to this truth. After we began to praise unitedly in our worship services, we had a great increase in the harvest results. Praise turned and softened hearts and prepared them for the richness of God's Word.

Hosea 11:12 informs us, "Judah yet ruleth with God, and is faithful with the saints." In this day when many are so caught up on authority, rulership, titles, and positions in the Body of Christ, it is refreshing to read that it is Praise that yet ruleth with God. We may not all come into an apostleship, but we can all come into praise and therein rule with God.

Joel 3:18 promises, "And it shall come to pass in that day, that ... all the rivers of Judah shall flow with waters, and a fountain shall come forth of the house of the Lord, and shall water the valley of Shittim." How true this is in today's move of the Spirit! Out from the midst of the people of praise there is flowing a fresh stream of the Holy Spirit that is irrigating the dry valleys of religion. Praise is not only the overflow of the Spirit, it is the source, the fountainhead of the Spirit's flow! Praise can cause a springing up of the waters of the Spirit after a parching day at the office, or in the home. Verse 20 adds,

"But Judah shall dwell [Hebrew abide] for ever and Jerusalem from generation to generation." Praise is not a novelty to the present charismatic move, any more than it was developed by the classic Pentecostals some seventy years ago. Praise always has been and always will be.

Malachi brings the Old Testament to a close, affirming, "Then shall the offering of Judah be pleasant unto the Lord, as in the days of old, and as in former years" (3:4). The first three verses of the third chapter speak of the dealings of the Lord in the lives of His people, and verse four gives the reason—that praise might be pleasant unto the Lord once again.

What a model, or paradigm, of praise is Judah! Imperfect, at times rebellious, sometimes hasty, sometimes slow, but intended to be a pleasant offering of praise unto the Lord.

Rituals of Worship, a Paradigm of Praise

God would not command His people to worship without giving them a pattern for worship. Inasmuch as praise is an integral part of worship, one would expect to find a pattern for praise woven into the required ritual, and it is there. Some people seem to feel that Old Testament worship was a dull routine of confession, slaughter of innocent animals, and fasting. This is not so at all. Far more of the worship was marked with rejoicing, thanksgiving, and feasting than with solemn fastings.

Take, for instance, the provision for the feasts. Three of these were compulsory, and each Hebrew male was required to return to Jerusalem for them. They were: (1) Feast of Passover (also called Feast of Unleavened Bread); (2) Feast of Pentecost (also called Feast of Weeks, Harvest, or First-Fruits); and (3) Feast of Tabernacles. In addition to these three compulsory feasts, two optional feasts were offered: (4) Feast of Trumpets, which formed the "New Year" of their civil year; and (5) The Feast of Atonement.

All these feasts were joyous occasions, regular family reunions. The sacrifices offered gave only a token part of the animal to the priest, and the rest was returned to the sacrificer for his part of the feast. It was somewhat like the old-fashioned "basket social" or the more recent pot-luck supper many of us have enjoyed. Then as now, eating, drinking, fellowshiping, and rejoicing were the keynotes of the day.

During the rebuilding of Jerusalem, its Temple, and its worship, Nehemiah and Ezra gathered the people into the street by the water gate and read God's law to them. Nehemiah 8:8-10, 12 records the reactions: "So they read in the book of the law of God distinctly, and gave the sense, and caused them to understand the reading. And Nehemiah ... and Ezra the priest the scribe, and the Levites that taught the people, said unto all the people, This day is holy unto the Lord your God; mourn not, nor weep. For all the people wept, when they heard the words of the law. Then he said unto them, Go your way, eat the fat, and drink the sweet, and send portions unto them for whom nothing is prepared: for this day is holy unto our Lord: neither be ye sorry; for the joy of the Lord is your strength. ... And all the people went their way to eat, and to drink, and to send portions, and to make great mirth, because they had understood the words that were declared unto them."

Such was the original way of celebrating the feasts of the Lord. While there is certainly a place for solemnity, there is equally a place for hilarity. There is a time for fasting but also a time for feasting; a time for judging and a time for joy. Once the Israelite had met God's requirements for sin, he was urged to rejoice in His saving God.

God's ordinances of worship began with a feast (Passover) and will end with a feast (Marriage Supper). The first was just before the Exodus, the second will be just after the entrance! In between the beginning and the end, there was a constancy of feasting before the Lord, for the feasts had three aspects to them:

(1) Past (a memorial), (2) Present (an experiential involvement for the individual), and (3) Future (prophetic of greater things to come).

And so there are three aspects of praise to the praiser. We praise as a memorial for His past doings, we praise because of a present involvement in His doings, and we praise because of a prophetic vision and hope. Whether looking backward, outward, or forward, we are motivated to praise the Lord, and feast before His presence with rejoicing and singing.

Take the provision made for a drink offering. This was not, as some have supposed, an offering of wine for the priest's consumption, for although our King James translation has named it a "drink offering," it was actually a "libation offering." The Hebrew word used here literally means "to pour out." It was an offering that was poured out before the Lord. It was not intended for man; it was presented to God.

This illustrates what happens in a man's spirit when he begins to praise. Something from deep within his spirit is "poured out" before the Lord. There is a flowing from him to God. Love, appreciation, adoration, and worship flow from his spirit, through the Holy Spirit, into the presence of God. It is not intended for man, nor is it presented to man. It is an offering from man's spirit to God.

A second offering worthy of note when considering praise was called the "heave offering." The Hebrew word signifies "a present or a gift." It is also translated, in the King James version, as a "freewill offering." All the gifts given for the construction of the tabernacle were called "heave offerings." These offerings were not required; they were totally "freewill" gifts unto God.

What a fitting symbol for what happens to a man's soul when he begins to praise! His emotions begin to open to God, his will responds to the urgings of his spirit, and he finds himself of his own free will giving praise, adulation, magnification, and exaltation to God with delight and pleasure. There is no pressure, no constraint, no coercion, for his soul "delights in the Lord his God." He finds himself joining David in crying, "Bless the Lord, O my soul: and all that is within me, bless his holy name" (Psalm 103:1).

Finally, a third offering worth remembering in this connection is called the "wave offering." In this offering, the priest took of the sacrifices of bread, cakes of meal, and shoulder of the ram and waved them before the Lord. The Hebrew word signifies, "shaking, waving, beckoning, or rocking to and fro." Exodus 29:24-25 tells us that after these offerings were waved before the Lord, they were to be burnt upon the altar "for a sweet savour before the Lord." But first, man's body was to get involved in waving it, shaking it, rocking it to and fro before the Lord.

I remember as a young boy seeing great congregations in camp meetings waving their hands before the Lord in praise and worship. Often they would take out their handkerchiefs, or lift a song book, and wave it before the Lord. I did not understand that they were simply entering into the "wave offering" that becomes a "sweet savour before the Lord" if offered in the fire of the Holy Spirit. It is difficult to get deeply involved in praise without having a physical participation in that praise. God not only expects, but anticipates and invites bodily participation. He views it as a "wave offering" before Him that will soon be consumed in the fire of His Spirit.

The "drink offering" illustrates the flowing out of man's spirit. The "heave offering" pictures the free will responding of man's soul, while the "wave offering" involves the man's body.

Praise is not confined to the heavens; it has been consigned to Earth. Although we see the divine pattern of praise in the heavens, we also see the divine model of praise on the Earth. In God's choice of Judah to exemplify and expound praise, we have paradigms of praise applied to the life of the individual believer.

In God's rituals of worship, both as to feasts and offerings, we see the extent of man's involvement in praise—spirit, soul, and body.

5

Persons in Praise

Standing behind the pulpit with my hands raised in praise one morning, I opened my eyes and was suddenly struck with the great diversity of manifestations. Some persons had their hands raised, others clasped their hands together. Some stood with bowed heads, while others had upturned faces. A few were kneeling, and there was a scattering of people seated, reading their Bibles. And it came to me: the church does not praise, individuals praise. Although united in a concept of adoration, our performances were very individualistic and personal.

My first impulse was to lead in a chorus to unite us in doing the same thing together. Then I realized how needless this would be, how typically this was me reacting in the flesh. We were united in praise, our thoughts were united on Jesus, it was only in our method of expression that each was "doing his own thing." The variety actually made it less ritualistic and more vital.

The comprehensive purpose for everything we had seen thus far was to involve people in praising the Lord. People praising—What of a few of the individuals in Scripture who represented a special group or class of people, who were worshipers and praisers?

Adam

The first man was Adam. The Bible tells us very little of what he said; however, we do know he had intimate, personal fellowship and communication with the Lord, for the Lord came down into Eden in the cool of the day to walk and talk with Adam (Genesis 3:8). Certainly this is the ultimate end of praise, to bring us into the divine presence.

Enoch

Of Enoch, Genesis 5:24 says, "Enoch walked with God: and he was not; for God took him." Again, praise's ultimate!

Noah

Noah also was brought into intimate communication and communion with God. After the flood, one of his first acts was to build an altar for worship (Genesis 8:20).

Abraham

The next emphasis of Scripture upon specific men is with the great patriarchs of old—Abraham, Isaac, and Jacob. Abraham was a man of the altar, a man of feasts, a man of prayer, a man of sacrifices, one who humbled himself before God. He was a man of faith, called in the Bible, "a friend of God" and "a righteous man." Jesus said of him, in John 8:56, "Abraham rejoiced to see my day."

Isaac

In sharp contrast with his father, Isaac seemed to be a quiet, peace loving man. The Scriptures tell us that God appeared to him, reaffirmed the Abrahamic covenant to him, blessed him, and that, under the blessing of God, Isaac blessed his two sons (Genesis 21-27). He was also known for re-digging his father's wells after the enemy had filled them (Genesis 26:15-18), much as the Spirit reopens the wells of our spirits after religion has filled them up. Praise needs the water of the Spirit and is willing to dig for it.

Jacob

Jacob was a true "character." Yet he was under the Abrahamic covenant, and God was faithful to him. Can we ever forget his great vision of the ladder stretched from Earth to Heaven with the angels of God ascending and descending on it? (Genesis 28:12). Jacob responded, upon awakening, by anointing a rock, the pillow upon which he had been sleeping (v. 18). It was Jacob, who upon returning to his own land, wrestled all night with an angel of God (Genesis 32:24-26). We see him before his altar and demanding purity of worship in his whole household. His relating to God finally changed his nature as well as his name (32:27-28). This is another purpose of praise, that we might be changed into His image.

Joseph

It was Jacob who, under the guidance of God, took the chosen family into Egypt where his long-lost son, Joseph, was a co-regent to the throne (Genesis 46). Who can fail to see that Joseph was a true worshiper of God, offering unto Him the praise of his life as well as his lips. In the midst of idol worship, he maintained true worship unto God, and even when standing before Pharaoh, who was himself looked upon as a God, Joseph proclaimed the name of Elohim!

Little of the speech of these brethren of old is recorded, but the fruit of their worship and praise is easily seen.

Moses

Four hundred years passed with virtually no history recorded in Scripture. Then God raised up a deliverer and lawgiver named Moses. Although God had to deal sorely and lengthily with him, no other man had such face-to-face communication with God, or was ever led so consistently by the supernatural hand of God. After the victorious crossing through the Red Sea, and the subsequent destruction of the enemy forces, Moses lifted his voice and began to sing a song of triumph that was both a proclamation and a prophecy.

Exodus 15 records the song. The first two verses declare, "Then sang Moses and the children of Israel this song unto the Lord, and spake, saying, I will sing unto the Lord, for he hath triumphed gloriously: the horse and his rider hath he thrown into the sea. The Lord is my strength and song, and he is become my salvation: he is my God, and I will prepare him an habitation: my father's God, and I will exalt him."

Moses' pledge to prepare God "an habitation" reveals his unusual understanding of praise, for as we have already seen, God inhabits the praises of Israel (Psalm 22:3). Revelation 15:3 tells us that after our victory is complete, and heaven is gained, we will join the great multitude on the sea of glass and sing the song of Moses! So great was the prophecy of Moses' praise, that it will suffice as a song of deliverance for us!

Melchizedek

One of the first provisions of the law, given through Moses, was for a priesthood. God had already revealed his acceptance of a priesthood long before Abraham's first son was born. Genesis 14:18-20 tells us, "And Melchizedek king of Salem brought forth bread and wine: and he was the priest of the most high God....And he...said, "Blessed be. . .the most high God, which hath delivered thine enemies into thy hand."

Aaron

When God began to reveal his design for a priesthood, he chose Aaron as the first high priest. He was to become a man of the altar, a man of the censer, the man who entered, annually, into the divine presence of the Holy of Holies. He it was who offered the wave offerings before the Lord and poured out the libation offerings as an act of worship. Little wonder, then, that Psalm 115:9 implored, "O house of Aaron, trust in the Lord." Years later the Psalmist pleaded with the progeny of Aaron to continue in blessing and praising the Lord: "Bless the Lord, O house of Aaron" (Psalm 135:19).

Deborah

For many years, the guidance for God's people came through the priesthood. The Book of Judges, however, records times of spiritual decline which encouraged Israel's enemies to rise up against them. Repeatedly, God raised up deliverers who became rulers under the title of "Judges." Many of these offered praise to God during times of victories, but the most outstanding praise comes from the lips of Deborah, who, with Barak, gained a rousing victory over the Canaanites. The song is recorded in Judges 5. Verses 2 and 9 highlight the song: "Praise ye the Lord for the avenging of Israel, when the people willingly offered themselves. ... My heart is toward the governors of Israel, that offered themselves willingly among the people. Bless ye the Lord."

Samuel

Following the rule of the judges was another period of rule by priests which ended with the godless rule of the household of Eli. Then Samuel took the reigns of leadership, functioning both as prophet and priest, living a life above reproach in its godliness and worship. Toward the end of his rule, the people demanded a king, and the rest of Israel's history is connected with kingly rulership.

David

As touching praise and worship, David was undoubtedly the most outstanding of all the kings of Judah and Israel. His Psalms have given rise to praise for many generations. We can hear David saying, "I will bless the Lord at all times: his praise shall continually be in my mouth. My soul shall make her boast in the Lord: the humble shall hear thereof, and be glad. O magnify the Lord with me, and let us exalt his name together" (Psalm 34:1-3).

David was not only a praiser himself, but he continually exhorted others to join him in praising the Lord. He taught singers to praise the Lord, he trained choirs and orchestras and appointed them to the service of praising the Lord twenty-four hours a day. He seldom lost sight of the fact that until the Lord came on the scene he was just a despised shepherd boy. He continually gave the glory to the Lord.

Isaiah

Concurrent with the reign of the kings was the reign of the prophets. They often played a pivotal role in the political as well as the spiritual affairs of the nation. They frequently were spiritual advisers to the throne, and in the case of Isaiah, a prophet was tutor to the king. The messages they received from God often became the guidelines for a generation.

Isaiah's writings are filled with praise. It was Isaiah who first saw into the heavens and witnessed divine praise. Little wonder, then, that he executed the commission that was born in praise, with much expression of praise. The entire twelfth chapter is a chapter of praise: "And in that day thou shalt say, O Lord, I will praise thee … Therefore with joy shall ye draw water out of the wells of salvation … Praise the Lord … make mention that his name is exalted. Sing unto the Lord … Cry out and shout, thou inhabitant of Zion: for great is the Holy One of Israel in the midst of thee." Isaiah 25:1 cries, "O Lord, thou art my God: I will exalt thee, I will praise thy name; for thou hast done wonderful things; thy counsels of old are faithfulness and truth." In 35:10, he promises, "And the ransomed of the Lord shall return, and come to Zion with songs and everlasting joy upon their heads: they shall obtain joy and gladness, and sorrow and sighing shall flee away." Isaiah 42:10 implores, "Sing unto the Lord a new song, and his praise from the end of the earth," while 43:21 declares, "This people have I formed for myself; they shall shew forth my praise."

Habakkuk

All of the minor prophets (minor meaning "briefer," not "less important") contain some message of praise. Noteworthy among them is Habakkuk. He begins his book with criticism of the ways of God and questions of "how long" (1:2), "why" (1:3), and "wherefore" (1:13). He seems to be at the end of his wavering faith, and goes to his prayer tower to seek a visitation from God. He ends the second chapter with, "But the Lord is in His holy temple: let all the earth keep silence before him" (2:20). The third chapter is a vocal embodiment of praise. It begins with, "His glory covered the heavens, and the earth was full of His praise" (3:3) and ends with, "Yet I will rejoice in the Lord, I will joy in the God of my salvation. The Lord God is my strength, and he will make my feet like hinds' feet, and he will make me to walk upon mine high places. To the chief singer on my stringed instruments (double harp)" (3:18-19).

This preferrer of charges against God becomes a proclaimer of praises unto God after a season in God's presence.

Jesus

In the New Testament, who can see Jesus without seeing praise? As soon as Mary was assured of her pregnancy, she burst forth into magnificent praise. The angels announced His birth with peals of praise. The shepherds observed the Christ-child with praise and wonderment. Men and women from all walks of life praised Him while He walked among them. He, himself, publicly gave thanks to the Father. Hebrews 2:12 quotes Him as saying, "I will declare thy name unto my brethren, in the midst of the church will I sing praise unto thee." Everything about Jesus spoke of praise; everything in His earthly life; from birth to death and Resurrection and ascension was attended and surrounded with praise!

Paul

Every New Testament book Paul authored, except Titus, which deals almost exclusively with church government, contains expressions of praise. He called for singing praise, rejoicing praise, praise of thanksgiving, sacrifice of praise, and the lifting up of hands in praise. Unquestionably, his heavy emphasis was, "Rejoice in the Lord." He exemplified his philosophy of praise in the Philippian jail when he and Silas began to sing praises unto God in the midst of the pain and persecution (Acts 16:25). He not only lectured on praise, he lived it as well!

John

That John the Beloved understood praise is more evident in his writing as the revelator than as the historian. His Book of Revelation is filled with multitudes praising the Lord. Who can read this book of "endings" without being caught up in the great wealth of praise and adoration that the ransomed pour out upon God and His Christ!

Such a fast walk through the Bible cannot hope to give a complete picture of the praisers of God whose names are recorded in Holy Writ, and is intended only to show how many more praisers there were than David and his Psalms. Every era of God's dealing with men has produced its praisers, and thank God that through His present dealings by His Spirit, the church is being reawakened to praise.

6

The Pact of Praise

"**N**ow if you will just sign here ... and here ... and here, it's all yours."

The widespread use of installment credit today makes us more aware of the power of a contract than ever before. When the first party has fulfilled certain stated obligations, the second party is bound, by this written covenant, to perform stated services. Once the parties have entered into the pact, it is enforceable by law. Society demands that the obligations be fulfilled, and this is the security of the covenant.

The Scriptures declare that in the life of the believer, praise is beautiful, necessary, and pleasing to God. But we sometimes fail to realize that praise is a pact, a covenant—not a covenant man makes with God, but a covenant that God has made with man. In Psalm 81, we have a recital of this pact of praise that God offers to His children.

Throughout the Old Testament, we distinguish God's covenants with Adam, Abraham, Jacob, Moses, David, and through the prophets, with His chosen people. In the New Testament, we find that both salvation and the infilling of the

Holy Spirit are covenant promises. Whenever God makes a covenant, He binds himself by the oath of His Word to fulfill His part; indeed, most of the basic benefits we derive from God are the result of a covenant that God has made with His people. The entire Old Testament is a covenant. "Testament" means "covenant" in modern English. The Old Testament is still called the "Old Covenant" in some translations of the Bible. It is the "old pact" God made with His people. At the Eucharist, Jesus said, "This cup is the new testament (covenant, pact) in my blood" (1 Corinthians 11:25).

The Old Covenant is not something Abraham made with God, but something God made with Abraham and many others; neither is the New Covenant something you make with God. The covenant is not in your submission to it; the covenant, He said, "is in My blood." It is true that if you would become a participant in the pact, there are certain things you must do, but your doing them does not produce the covenant—it only makes the covenant valid for you because you have met the pre-existing conditions of the pact.

Psalm 81 gives us the concept of God making a pact or entering into a covenant with His people. "Hear, O my people, and I will testify unto thee: O Israel, if thou wilt hearken unto me ..." (v. 8).

In this Psalm, God is stating previous promises made and is making a record of them or reiterating them as a legal witness for all to see. The strong implication is the making of a "testament" or entering into a pact or covenant in the matter of praise. "Hear (and heed) my people, and I will make a testament, covenant, pact with thee."

Covenants are generally conditional: "If you'll do this, I'll do that." When we buy a car or a house, and need financing, we sign a contract or pact wherein we agree to make regular payments of a specified amount, and the other party agrees to let us have possession of the property and later, upon completion of our payment schedule, full title to it. It is an "I will if you will" pact or contract. This is so with God's covenants. He says, "If My people will—I will … "

The pact presented in Psalm 81 suggests, first, the conditions that must be met in order to enter into the covenant, and then lists God's promises or pledges to the person who will meet the conditions. The final three verses give some covenant benefits, or five things that accrue to the person of the pact.

Our side of this pact is given in the first seven verses. Five methods of praise and five motivations for praise are spelled out, and unless we fulfill the basic condition—praising God—we will be cheated out of the benefits of this covenant of praise. (See chapter seven, "The Performance of Praise," for a discussion of methods of praise.)

In the New Testament, we find an interesting verse which is not usually quoted in its entirety. In 1 Peter 2:9, we read, "But ye are a chosen generation, a royal priesthood, an holy nation, a peculiar people." This is where we usually stop, but it is not where the verse stops. What it says after the semicolon is: "That ye should show forth the praises of him who hath called you out of darkness into his marvellous light." For this He has called us. For this He has made priests of us. For this we are peculiar and different. That we might get together to show forth His praise.

The covenant condition, therefore, is obviously praise. As we praise Him, He moves toward us. But, you may ask, what is a proper motivation for praise? Is it proper to praise just so I can get something from God? What should a Christian's motivation be for praising the Lord? In Psalm 81:4-7, the Holy Spirit gives us six strong reasons for praise, reasons we can understand and relate to, reasons that combine the dealings of God with the deliverance of man.

The first reason for praise is given in verse four: "For this was a statute … and a law of the God of Jacob." This alone should be sufficient. God's Word commands it! Note that it is not listed as an option for those who want a deeper experience with God; it is given as a repeated command.

"Praise ye the Lord" means, "All ye people praise the Lord." Psalm 47:1 declares, "O clap your hands all ye people," while Psalm 40:16 says, "Let all those that seek thee rejoice and be glad in thee." This is the word of the King of kings and Lord of lords. Refusal to praise is rebellion against God's Word.

The second reason for praise is that praising people are God's testimony. "This he ordained in Joseph for a testimony" (Psalm 81:5). The cornerstones of many of our massive cathedrals dedicate the building, "To the Glory of God," and much of the greatest music ever written has been inscribed, "To the Glory of God." Yet the Bible teaches that "We should be to the praise of his glory, who first trusted in Christ" (Ephesians 1:12). Jesus said, "Ye shall be my witnesses."

Contrary to a prevalent belief among many new charismatic Christians, it is not the demonstration of power that God has chosen as a testimony unto himself, but a declaration of Praise! Praise is a testimony unto God understood both in the heavens and on the Earth. As a matter of fact, it is dangerous to get very involved in a display of divine power until you are well entrenched in praise. I've seen what the misuse of spiritual gifts can do to destroy an individual or a church by bringing them into high pride levels. Praise, on the other hand, is conducive to humility, for the only direction praise can go is upward. Until we have learned to worship and praise, we do well to shy away from the power. Where there are people who will praise, there is testimony of Christ; the expressed attitudes have been to Him. He is center and paramount. Then out of this atmosphere of praise, we can safely release the divine power to minister to the needs of people. Let's have the adoration of Jesus first, then the authority of Jesus can safely follow. Praise, then power!

A further reason for praise is our deliverance from slavery.

"I removed his shoulder from the burden: his hands were delivered from the pots. Thou calledst in trouble, and I delivered thee" (Psalm 81:6-7). How this thought should produce praise! God freed and delivered His people. And He is in the same business today. Slaves are still being transformed into free men. Hallelujah!

In Egypt, the people were the servile vassals of their captors. Their tasks included carrying all the burdens—they were treated much the same as beasts of burden. Their hands were constantly "in the pots," both in cooking and cleaning.

Then the Lord delivered them, and just listen to Miriam with her tambourine leading the women in response to the song of Moses in Exodus 15.

Are you losing your own desire to praise? Bring to remembrance exactly where and what you were before knowing the deliverance and security found in Jesus Christ. Take another look at some of the scenes you were a part of when you were a servant of sin. Are you glad to be free? Tell Him so.

Not only has God delivered His people from the slavery of sin, He is also delivering them from servitude to "religion." I use the word in a negative sense, as Moffatt translates it, having a form but no force ["Though they keep up a form of religion, they will have nothing to do with it as a force" (2 Timothy 3:5)].

Other than Satan himself, there is probably no sterner taskmaster than organized religion. It often forces us to carry burdens that are not our own—to stir pots for other people. If God has delivered you from bearing the burden of "need orientation," praise Him for it. If the Lord, in His grace, has delivered you from ceaseless toil in the pot of "the denomination," freeing you to be involved in the things of God, praise Him for it. If you have found relationship with Christ instead of dead ritual, praise Him for it. We do well to remember our deliverances, mark them upon our foreheads, recite them unto our children, use them as reason for praise day and night. We were bondsmen, we were slaves, and He has delivered us! (Rest assured that I am speaking of a lifeless "religion" that substitutes itself for a relationship with God. I am not against organization or churches, nor dare I be, for God and His Word are for them.)

A fourth reason for praising the Lord is, "I answered thee" (v. 7). Not only were the people delivered from slavery, but they barely got across the Red Sea before God started answering their prayers. There was the request for sweet water and manna. He provided for their every need when they called upon Him. They should never have lost the awe they felt as God performed miracle after miracle in their behalf.

What about us today? Do we still feel a sense of awe as we think about the God of all the universe listening to our prayers and answering them? Who am I that the King of kings should pause and listen, much less pay attention and answer me. Here am I, one infinitesimal segment of society. I cry, "Oh, God, for Jesus' sake, will You do this for me?" And He answers. If that cannot evoke a sense of wonder and response of praise, then somewhere along the line I have forgotten my relationship and think I deserve this response.

There is a prayer that often comes from my lips: "Thank You, God, that I do not get what I deserve." I do not ever want what I deserve. I am grateful that God has offered me grace, not justice. God listens when I pray. And consistent with His will, He answers. Let that thought evoke praise within you! Praise Him for answered prayer whether the answer was, "Yes," "No," "Later," or "I will if you will."

We often fail to praise the Lord for His provings, testings, trials, and temptations, yet the fifth reason given for praise is, "I proved thee" (Psalm 81:7). We fail to realize that God never tests our weak points, only our strong ones. "I will test my man to reveal what I have put in him." Satan likes to present the situation to us as a temptation, and we often refer to the same situation as a trial. But God says, "Call it a temptation or call it a trial, I initiated it as a test."

Now why does God test us? For the same reason that a manufacturer tests a new product before a new product is put on the market. After many and varied testings, the laboratory writes a certified report to the manufacturer saying, "You can easily guarantee that this product will take seventy years of normal usage. We have abused it far beyond that point." So the advertisement declares, "Lifetime Guarantee." How dare they do this? They have put it to the test and discovered its strength. God does that with you. He wants you to discover how great is His strength within your life.

Have you ever tripped and fallen flat on your face on what you thought was one of your "strong points"? This seems to be where I fall. When I think I am strong, then I am weak. Then the grace of God comes, and God begins doing a work in me. He cleanses me and stands me up in His faith again. But from that time on, I am very apprehensive about a repeat situation. One day I may be brought right into the presence of the same "trial" or "temptation," and there seems to be no escape. My heart cries, "Oh, God, not again!" All the while, the devil is whispering in my ear, "This is the end. You've had it!"

Suddenly I find myself moving right on out of the situation, as if it were not even there. As I look back in amazement, I say, "I did not fail. In fact, it did not even bother me. Oh, Lord, thank you." The Lord replies, "The reason for the test is to let you know that I have been building strength in you, that My grace is sufficient and you need not live in fear. I have proved you."

Can you identify with the Psalmist as he cries, "The Lord is my strength ... The Lord is my rock ... The Lord is my shield ... The Lord is my reward ... The Lord is my buckler ... The Lord is my high tower"? You are strong in the Lord! How did you find out? Because He tested you, because the devil tempted you, because you were terribly tried and came forth as pure gold. He wants you to praise Him for that. You would never know the strengths within you if He didn't test you once in a while.

Our part of the pact, then, is simply to praise the Lord! Verse eight of this 81st Psalm ends, "If thou wilt hearken unto me." What has He been talking about? Praise! You dare not apply this statement to the law, ordinances, commandments, or statutes, for that would take the verse completely out of context.

What God has been asking for is praise; He has been talking about praise. He simply says, "If you will, I will." If you will praise, I will ... and in verses 9-10 He lists four things He will do. These are the promises of this pact or covenant.

"There shall no strange god be in thee." Through the Old Testament, "strange gods" is merely a euphemism for "demons." Behind all idolatry is demonic power. Men think they are bowing to stone or silver images, but demons accept it as direct worship to themselves. Little wonder that God is so opposed to idolatry of any kind.

Moreover, we are living today in the midst of an occult explosion. Since there has also been a restoration of the ministry of exorcism to the church, many believing Christians have become unduly demon conscious and live in the mistaken fear of becoming inhabited by alien forces themselves. How reassuring that the first provision of this pact made by God is that He will be our protection from all Satanic attack!

Deuteronomy 32:9-18 reveals why some Christians have trouble with the Satanic and others do not. To me, this passage coincides beautifully with this first promise of the pact of praise. Verse nine informs us, "For the Lord's portion is his people." Without us, He has no inheritance. The tenth verse tells us that God found them, led them, instructed them, and protected them as He would the "apple (pupil TAB) of his eye." Verse 12 says, "So the Lord alone did lead them, and there was no strange god with him." As long as we stay in a praising relationship, we have the assurance of this covenant that God will secure total protection from the Satanic for the children of His inheritance.

Deuteronomy 32:13-14 shows how God's provision for His people is more than ample, it is luxurious. "It is your Father's good pleasure to give you the kingdom" (Luke 12:32). Verse 15, however, says that after these people were totally satisfied and had actually gotten "fat" on God's provision, they began a four-step, downward progression that moved them from the realms of the divine to the demonic.

First, they "forsook God" (Deuteronomy 32:15). This was one of God's complaints throughout the Old Testament. As long as He blessed His people with abundance, they tended to forsake Him. When He sold them into bondage, they called on His name. How God yearns to give us the best of everything, but He fears it will cause us to rise in self-will and self-love instead of praise … to forsake rather than to follow … to become self-oriented instead of God-centered. Is it not easy to become gift-oriented, or power-centered or structure-conscious the moment God begins to share His divine provisions with us? While none of these things are necessarily evil in themselves, if they replace the affection we once had for God, if they occupy our attention, we are "forsaking God" just as much as the man who seeks to return to "the pleasures of this world."

After forsaking God, the second step (Deuteronomy 32:16) was, "They provoked him to jealousy with strange gods." I've seen this pattern repeated often in my years of ministry. People come through redemption, into praise, then on to provision until they start getting fat on the provision of the Lord. Then they start looking around for something new, a new "kick," and faster than you might realize it, they're playing the "demonology game." They, like the disciples of old, are excited because "even the devils are subject unto us." [I wonder if the sharp rebuke that Christ gave His disciples for that prideful report wouldn't do our generation of "demon-chasers" some good: "Rejoice not, that the spirits are subject unto you; but rather rejoice, because your names are written in heaven" (Luke 10:20)].

God warned His people, in His very first visitation at Sinai, that He was a "jealous God;" that He would tolerate no other gods before Himself. Happy is the saint who learns, early in his walk, not to try to mix the divine and the demonic—the light and the darkness; not to share his attention and affections with both.

The next step downward is, "They sacrificed unto devils, not to God (Deuteronomy 32:17). Sadly does 2 Kings 17:33 report, "They feared the Lord, and served their own gods." We may never lose our reverential respect for God, we may still maintain a love for Him, but where are we investing our lives? It is a short step from "playing" with strange gods to "sacrificing" unto them; from curiously reading about the occult to actively experimenting in it.

Nor is the use of idolatry limited to the strict literal sense: are we also serving Mammon, the god of affluence? What investment do we have in the gods of success, recognition, possessive love? What gods are we allowing to insinuate themselves between us and our God?

The final step is, "Thou ... hast forgotten God that formed thee" (Deuteronomy 32:18). By four restoring steps, God had brought them to a place where "there was no strange god with him." By four rebellious steps they had taken themselves away from God into the demonic realms. It is an easy, age-old progression: we tend to forsake God when we do not feel that we need Him. Very few people seek God because they want Him—they seek Him because they need Him. That is why He created need levels in us.

Amazingly, when we become interested in strange things, we begin to make sacrifices to follow this interest. They soon become part of us, and we fall into a total forgetting of God. The greatest protection anyone has from the Satanic is to keep your mind on God: "Thou wilt keep him in perfect peace, whose mind is stayed on thee" (Isaiah 26:3).

The second promise of this pact of praise is concerned with purity of worship. Psalm 81:9 pledges, "Neither shalt thou worship any strange god." Not only is divine protection offered to the praiser, but purity in his worship is equally assured. We will never be able to develop purity in worship because we are pure, but because He is going to take care of the purification. He and He alone can cleanse the impure motives from our lives, and keep our worship Christ-centered rather than church- , self- or program-centered.

Isaiah 43:12 states, "I have declared, and have saved, and I have shewed, when there was no strange god among you: therefore ye are my witnesses, saith the Lord, that I am God." When God has a Divine monopoly in our midst, He will declare, deliver, and demonstrate. But when we bring in a second "god," be it of self or of Satan, God withdraws from the scene and no longer speaks, saves, or shows. As R.A. Torrey used to say, "God will be Lord of all or not at all."

But how will we maintain such a realm of purity? We all have our selfish motivations, our self-love, our self-will. The answer is simply to praise God, and He will keep us pure. If there is to be any purity in our worship, it is going to be because we have given ourselves to the covenant of praise—we have accepted God's pact and are not trying to formulate one ourselves.

With real sorrow, I remember a dealing of God in my life some time ago while I was pastoring a church in Eugene, Oregon. In searching for greater reality than the denominational approach had brought to us, we found ourselves involved in casting out demons. We were very successful in it, although this was years ahead of the present emphasis that is becoming so popular. We soon discovered, however, that if you stir the demonic pot during the week, you can expect the services to be really boiling with demonic powers on Sunday. Week after week my associate pastor would struggle with a song service, finally signaling me for help. I would walk to the pulpit, ask for all heads to be bowed, eyes closed, and I would command the demon forces to leave the building. Almost immediately, there was a release in the midst, and the service could proceed unhindered. However, we usually had to repeat the performance for the evening service and the midweek sessions.

One morning, as I was in prayer, the Lord spoke to me and said, "My son, I would be first in your church." I quickly responded, "But, Lord, You always have top billing. You are Number One in this church. You are the center of our song and sermon. No one is above You in our affections or worship."

But the Lord said, "You do not lead your people to worship Me until you have led them in the worship of demons."

"Not so, Lord," I cried. "Far be it from me to bow my knee to a demon, much less lead a congregation in such worship.

He continued, "Each service you stand before your people and request that they bow their heads before the demons who are present, close their eyes in respect to them, and then you begin to talk to the demon forces. Their world accepts this as worship. Demon forces from far and near attend your services, for they have heard they will be worshiped if they come."

You can well imagine how this broke my heart. I was appalled to think that I had led the saints in the worship of demons. After much weeping and repenting, I asked the Lord what I should do.

He said, "Just ignore the presence of the demonic. Praise and worship Me. You are My people; this house has been dedicated unto the worship of Me. Center your people in praising Me, and I will deal with the demonic."

The following Sunday morning, I had hoped there would be a great liberty of worship. I had prayed much and pled with God to take care of the bondage. The service, however, was even more bound than usual. The song leader asked me to intervene. The moment I stepped into the pulpit, every head bowed and eyes closed, for this was the way I had trained them. This time, I asked them to look at me, and when I had finally gained their full attention, I said, "Isn't it wonderful that Jesus is here in such a glorious way?" They looked at one another as though I had gone crazy. I repeated it, but got no positive response.

I said, "Let us praise the Lord." They tried, but could not. Then I called them to the front of the church and told them that we would not deal with the demonic interference anymore; we were going to "major in God" and let Him take care of any opposition. It took quite a time, but finally the congregation broke through in praise, and when they did, real liberation came. From that day to the day I resigned as pastor of the assembly, we never publicly acknowledged the presence of demonic forces. We began every service with praise, and the Lord Jesus broke whatever bondage there may have been. Once the evil spirit forces were convinced that their days of being worshiped were over, once they knew that they could no longer hold our attention, they left. And they did not return. The answer to purity in worship is the same now as it was in Moses' day:

"If you will praise me, thou shalt not worship any strange God." Jesus still cleanses the temple when He comes in, and I'll tell you something: I can't prove it, but I suspect that the sweet aroma of heavenward praise is as acrid in the nostrils of Satan and his hordes as sulphur and brimstone are in ours. I'll just bet they can't stand it!

The third promise of this pact of praise is personal relationship. Psalm 81:10 says, "I am the Lord thy God." How does one come into this relationship? As you begin to praise God, something wonderful happens to your confidence in your relationship with God. You become aware that He is, in fact, what you are declaring—your Lord. There is a drawing of your spirit and His Spirit together. This strengthens your faith, your worship, your whole being, to know that God is intimately related to you. "I am thy God."

How desperately this is needed today. Only when we are secure in our own relationship to Jesus are we able to offer Jesus to anyone else. We may seek security in relationships in our families, our church, our friends. We may feel secure knowing they are interceding for us. But it is only as we come into the realization of His desire to be our sufficiency, that we can find complete freedom in our relationship with Him. This security is not dependent upon the people we are with, or the culture, or the circumstances. As we praise Him, we come into this glorious closeness and comfort.

And there's something else that happens in our relationship with Him when we start to praise. If there has been a hardness of heart on our part, a root of bitterness that has effectively blocked whatever He might have wanted to do on our behalf, there is nothing like praise to change one's heart attitude, soften one generally, and set into motion all that divine machinery which is just poised and waiting. Some of the hardest times to praise—when praise began through gritted teeth in blind obedience to the commands of Scripture—have ended in the greatest victory.

We must never forget that we did not choose Him. He chose us, ordained us, set us as a testimony, and revealed His grace through us to a sinful world. He has put His name on us, His nature within us, His Word in our heart, and His praise in our mouth. The whole spectrum of our intimate relationship with Him is what He has done. It is completed. He simply asks us to praise Him and thereby enter into the fullness of this personal relationship. He is not just the Redeemer, Creator, Lord of the universe; He is your Savior, your Lord, your Bridegroom, your soon-coming King. Hallelujah!

The fourth promise is certainly a manifestation of divine grace. "Open thy mouth wide, and I will fill it" (Psalm 81:10). With what will He fill our mouth? What has He been talking about in the whole Psalm? Praise! So, not only does He set praise as the condition we must meet to gain the benefits of this pact, He himself then supplies that praise. It is one of the promises of the covenant.

This reminds me of my situation as a father. When my daughters were small, they occasionally needed money to buy me a gift. They would approach me and, in their child like way, get across the message that they needed some money. I was not supposed to know that they were going to buy me a gift. So I gave them the money, and their need was met. The point is, they could not give "unto," until they had received "from." There was no other source of supply for them. Their joy in bringing me their gift was not lessened because they had to come to me as their source of supply. In fact, it tied us more closely together. This is what God wants. He yearns for a praising people. He is willing to meet our needs by giving us the praise so that our needs are again met as we give that praise to Him.

This provision is consistent with an equation found throughout the Scriptures: if you cannot come to God with what He requires, come to Him for what He requires. Before forgiveness, we are told to bring repentance to God. Sometimes we do not have a genuine repentance. Yet the New Testament tells us that repentance itself is a gift of God: "In meekness instructing those that oppose themselves; if God peradventure will give them repentance to the acknowledging of the truth" (2 Timothy 2:25).

We are told that without faith it is impossible to please God, but who among us can produce faith? Praise God, none of us needs to, for faith also is spoken of as a gift of God: "God hath dealt to every man the measure of faith" (Romans 12:3); "Faith cometh by hearing, and hearing by the word of God" (Romans 10:17); and "To them that have obtained like precious faith with us through the righteousness of God and our Saviour Jesus Christ" (2 Pet. 1:1). So if you cannot come to God with praise, come to God for praise, but come with a mouth wide open! He will fill it for you.

It is unfortunate that the next three verses of this Psalm had to be written. It would be glorious if the Psalmist could tell us that God's people did, in fact, become praising people and enjoyed all the benefits of this glorious covenant. But historically, each succeeding group of "called out ones" have embraced the covenant of praise for only brief periods of their early history and then turned to their own ways, methods, ideas, and programs. Psalm 81:11 sadly reports, "But my people [1] would not hearken to my voice; and [2] Israel would none of me." The voice of God ignored, the presence of God rejected! "So [1] I gave them up unto their own hearts' lust: and [2] they walked in their own counsels" (Psalm 81:12). God's punishment was simply to let them have their own way—and have it, and have it. If we won't walk after God's heart, He lets us walk after our own heart's desires. If we won't hearken to His voice, He lets us walk according to our own voice, and what desperate consequences accrue. The moment we feel that we can "do it," God stops doing. If we're going to be our own defense, God will get out of the way.

Like little children who do not want to do as they are told but want to do what the parents are doing, we seek to usurp God's authority and expressed responsibility and to do His work for Him. We feel that the part He has asked us to play is "beneath our dignity," below our maturity level, or demeaning to our station in life.

As we look at the closing verses of this Psalm, we cannot

help but sense the pathos as God says, "Oh that my people had hearkened...and...walked in my ways! I had purposed good things for them." Then are listed five covenant benefits that could have been theirs.

"I should soon have subdued their enemies" (Psalm 81:14). It was God's desire to bring them into rest, to deliver them from their struggles. But we cannot enter into that rest until we have ceased from our own labors. As long as we are going to do it, God will not do it. But if we are going to let God do it, we do not have to do it.

Speaking to religious people of His day, Jesus said, "Come unto me, all ye that labour and are heavy laden, and I will give you rest. Take my yoke upon you, and learn of me; for I am meek and lowly in heart: and ye shall find rest unto your souls" (Matthew 11:28-29).

For years I could not understand this. When I am worn out, the last thing I want to do is stick my neck in a yoke. What did Jesus mean? Meditating on a yoke of oxen, I found that when you get your neck in His yoke, you will begin to learn. You will learn that if you try to go before He goes, all you are going to get is sore shoulders. You will learn that if you refuse to go when He goes, you are going to have sore ears. You will find that when He turns left and you do not want to turn in that direction, you will get a real crick in the side of your neck. You will learn to eat when He eats, because that is the only time the neck yoke goes down. You will find one of the most glorious lessons to be learned—that your job is simply to hold up your end of the yoke. He will do the pulling. If you are yoked with Him, you will realize that you are just going along for the walk—you are there to learn, not to work. There is a rest. We do become a participant, but it is His work, His way, His will, His time, and His place. You will learn that a result of praise will be a contentment in moving with God because you are beginning to really know Him.

The second provision of covenant blessing would have been divine battling. "I should soon have … turned my hand against their adversaries" (Psalm 81:14). It is a marvelous thing when God undertakes against our adversaries, and we do have them, in the flesh and in the spiritual realm. Do not pick up the closest tool at hand and go to battle. Praise the Lord, and He will turn His hand against them.

Some years ago when I first began ministering on foreign soil, the Lord gave a beautiful vision to a brother in my congregation. He saw God lowering a dome-shaped canopy of glass over me as hordes of demon powers came against me, and they just hit the glass and bounced off. Later, I went to an area of ministry and faced a great demonic force in the community. To my rejoicing, the vision was fulfilled. I was gloriously protected, untouchable because of His "hand" that was for me and against them.

There is a beautiful truth in Psalm 8:2: "Out of the mouth of babes and sucklings hast thou ordained strength because of thine enemies, that thou mightest still the enemy and the avenger." Jesus quotes this in Matthew 21:16, but He changes two words. Instead of "Thou hast ordained strength," He says, "Thou hast perfected praise. " Using the "Jesus translation," look at the verse again. "Out of the mouth of babes and sucklings hast thou perfected praise because of thine enemies, that thou mightest still the enemy and the avenger." Could anything be presented more clearly? God has perfected the pattern of praise as a powerful weapon against the enemy. As we praise, God's hand moves against them.

The third benefit of this pact is the pledge that our victories would be perpetuated. "The haters of the Lord should have submitted themselves unto Him: but their time (the Berkeley translation adds 'of retribution') should have endured forever" (Psalm 81:15). I cannot perpetuate spiritual victories. I may win one, but I will have to fight it again and again. In desperation

I cry out, "My God, what can I do?" He replies, "Let Me perpetuate the victory." This, too, is part of this covenant of praise: what He provides, He perpetuates!

The fourth provision is given as, "He should have fed them also with the finest of the wheat" (Psalm 81:16). God chooses to give the very best to His children, yet we spend so much of our time struggling and grasping to provide for ourselves. As we fulfill our part of the covenant, we find Him amply filling His part, providing for our every need—spirit, soul, and body—with the very finest possible joys and blessings.

The final provision is also in verse 16: "And with honey out of the rock should I have satisfied thee." Satisfaction! How we search and strive for it. And all of the time God is waiting to give us complete satisfaction in every area of life. Picture after picture is painted in the Old Testament of the struggles of the Israelites to find satisfaction. They turned to strange gods for religious satisfaction; they turned to foreign practices and people for answers to their physical needs. Yet all the time God was reaching out toward them with His hands full of the good things which were their rightful inheritance as His children. But instead of just praising God as He had commanded, and partaking of his bountiful supply, they sought after broken cisterns that could not possibly hold water. They spent time and money for things which could not fully satisfy—exchanging the lasting things of God for temporary pleasures.

Full satisfaction is to be found in being like Jesus. Although we have not yet attained the fullness of Christ, the Holy Spirit is at work in us at the present, seeking to produce the divine image in us. 2 Corinthians 3:18 reminds us, "But we all, with open face beholding as in a glass the glory of the Lord, are changed into the same image from glory to glory, even as by the Spirit of the Lord." Is there any time in our Christian discipline when we behold the face of the Lord more than during praise? Is that not one of the prerequisites of praise, that we look away from ourself and see Him? It is in this seeing that we are changed into His image. "Beloved, now are we the sons of God, and it doth not yet appear what we shall be: but we know that, when he shall appear, we shall be like him; for we shall see him as he is" (1 John 3:2).

Read again the 81st Psalm in its entirety. Read it as a pact or covenant that God is presenting to you. He has signed it for eternity in the blood of His Son, Jesus Christ. Will you sign your name as party of the second part?

7

The Performance of Praise

Probably the most important instruction in praise given in the entire Bible is given in the first four words of Psalm 149. "Praise ye the Lord." This is, of course, a translation of the Hebrew words Haw-lai jah (our "hallelujah"), but we need to realize that the injunction of the Word is more than simply to praise the Lord; it is for you to praise the Lord.

So often, as I have ministered in camp meetings, conferences, retreats, and conventions, people have told me that if they could have been a member of my congregation on the West Coast, they, too, would be praisers. I have regularly told them that long before the Lord requires congregational praise, He calls for personal, individual praise. Whether your church praises the Lord or not, "Praise ye the Lord." Whether your prayer group or house meeting gives time for vocal expression of praise or not, "Praise ye the Lord."

Praise is not a mass function, it is the response of an individual to his God. When a group of individuals choose to unite in praising, their individual praises may blend into a group response, but every expression of the praise comes from a separate individual. My response to God need not be affected by another's response or their lack of response. Since my salvation, my free moral agency has been returned to me; I am an individual in my own right, and if I choose to exercise my will, I can praise the Lord, regardless of the pattern of behavior of those around me.

Don't blame the pastor for lack of praise, don't blame the denomination for praise-lessness, "Praise ye the Lord." You don't have to be led in praise, you don't even need emotional stimuli, just raise your hands and "Praise ye the Lord." Some of Scripture's greatest praisers praised in spite of circumstances and as a solo performance. Once we have learned to praise as individuals, we'll have little difficulty participating in group praise. So say it, sing it, share it, show it, shout it, or strum it—but start it! Determine that you will praise the Lord!

Often we have difficulty voicing our praise for lack of vocabulary. "Okay, I'm willing to praise the Lord. I really want to, but how do I begin? What do I say?"

God has provided for that contingency. Those of us who have never uttered one word of praise before can begin to praise by using the praises of the great praisers. When you read, "Bless the Lord, O my soul, and forget not all His benefits," you can say, "That's the way I feel about it, too." As you read the words of John, "Worthy is the Lamb," you can add, "Amen, that's what I'm trying to say!"

At times when I was more confused than filled with joy, I have taken the Psalms and read them aloud unto God. As my spirit began to respond to the Words of God's Spirit, there was a lifting that brought rejoicing and victory. Using God's own Words is a marvelous route to high-level praise.

The second instruction about praise, as listed in Psalm 149, is, "Sing unto the Lord a new song" (v. 1). Not many of our major modes of worship and praise are mentioned as often in the Bible as singing. There are more than three hundred injunctions scattered throughout the Scriptures that tell us to sing. Singing played an important part in the Hebrew worship. When David returned the Ark to Jerusalem, he appointed singers and provided that singing should be done before the Ark day and night. "And these are they whom David set over the service of song in the house of the Lord, after that the ark had rest. And they ministered...with singing" (1 Chronicles 6:31-32). First Chronicles 9:33 adds, "They were employed in that work day and night."

Almost every great general in history knew the tremendous power of song. When the pressure was greatest and fear was rampant, Jehoshaphat caused his troops to begin to sing (2 Chronicles 20). How many times has a seemingly beaten body of men been rallied and given new heart by the singing of a beloved marching song or battle hymn? And not just rallied, but transformed? General Booth, the founder of the Salvation Army, once said, "Who said the devil had all the good music?" and countless sidewalk bands in red and blue have known the power of stirring gospel music.

Singing has traditionally been one of the Christian's secret weapons. The martyrs in the arena, faced with being torn apart by wild animals, came out singing. Corrie ten Boom, in solitary confinement, began each day by singing "Stand Up, Stand Up for Jesus."

I myself have seen congregations gripped with fear and unbelief begin to sing. Soon they sing themselves into reception of faith and then into a release of that faith. They sing themselves from darkness to light, from defeat to victory.

Every revival the world has known has been accompanied with singing. True, in many churches the singing is by remote identification: the choir sings and the people say amen. But where there is a fresh moving of God, people sing because they want to express something within toward God.

Praising in song performs at least three valuable things for the praiser. First, it affords him a ready-made praise vocabulary. When we begin to sing songs of praise, we have before us words that have been meaningful to others and with which we can easily relate. Some songs have been born in the midst of great experiences with God, and the very singing of them allows us to identify with a high level of praise expression.

Singing praise also contributes to a unity in our response. David was always urging others to join him in praising the Lord. The greater the awareness of God and His glory, the greater the desire to join others or have them join us in lauding that glorious Lord. In song, there is a quick uniting of hearts in praise. We are singing the same words, at the same tempo, to the same tune at the same time, and the cumulative effect is often dynamic! Even if we are singing alone, there is still the sense of uniting with the author and with many others who have, in times past, sung the same song.

A third value of praising in singing is that it helps release the inner emotions that have often been locked up behind the veneer of our culture. For instance, men are taught that it is unmanly for them to weep or show tenderness. In learning to repress weeping, they usually repress all expression of tenderness as well. They find expression in "manly" ways that are acceptable to our culture. Yet boisterous behavior, kidding, physical aggressiveness, and so on, are not conducive to praise. When men and women begin to sing with understanding and anointing, they often find a release for the emotions that is acceptable both to themselves and to their peers, and to God.

Eight separate Hebrew words in the Old Testament are translated "sing" in the King James version of the Bible. According to James Strong's Hebrew dictionary, (appended to his complete concordance to the Bible), the definitions of these words indicate that singing in Old Testament times was more than the sweet, melodious choral and congregational singing of our churches. One of these words means "to shout or sing aloud for joy." Another, "a shrill sound, or a shout of gladness and rejoicing." Yet another, "joyful voice singing and triumphing," while still another suggests the idea of a strolling minstrel.

Obviously, then, there was a releasing of joyful, triumphant, shouting emotions when the people were singing unto Jehovah. I believe that singing praise will always have some of these factors in it. Congregations have sung together for years and never gotten involved in praise, but when they do get involved, their singing seems not only to come alive, but to explode with emotion.

"Sing unto God. Sing praises to his name" (Psalm 68:4). Don't sing songs; sing praises—with your mind on the meaning of the words, and your heart in them. Don't sing to people; sing to the Lord. Don't concentrate on musical perfection; concentrate on releasing your inner self in the song. For singing to be praise, the praiser must consciously be singing the song about the Lord or unto the Lord. Not all songs lend themselves to praiseful singing. They should have a Christ-centeredness, either as to His nature and person or as to what He has done. Even songs that are testimony-oriented can be songs of praise if we are less conscious of what we have become and more conscious of all that He has done for and in us.

Just as it helps to create a mental image when talking to someone on the phone, lest you become impersonal in your communication, so it is necessary to have some mental image of the person to whom you are speaking when singing praises. Don't just sing into the air; mentally place yourself in direct communication with God and sing unto Him.

In Hebrews 2:12 Christ is quoted as saying, "I will declare thy name unto my brethren, in the midst of the church will I sing praise unto thee." The Greek word used for "sings" is humneo, from which we derive our word hymn. It means to sing a religious ode or to celebrate God in song. If this is the type of singing Jesus uses for praising, we would do well to emulate Him.

As valuable as it is for us to use the songs of others, while learning a praise vocabulary, the Spirit within us would like to release the singing of a "new song"—that which is particularly expressive of you and your experience. Don't hesitate in releasing new songs during your praise time. God delights in hearing the "new song." For instance, in the present move of God there is a good deal of emphasis on singing Scriptures.

Singing the Scriptures can become double-praising. There is the melodious release of the inner feelings plus the anointed words of the Bible. What melody? Well, there are many traditional tunes, but if you don't happen to know any, just lean out on the Holy Spirit. Start, and see what happens. You may be very happily surprised! When I begin singing the 150th Psalm, I start to feel what the author felt and to sense and see what he was experiencing, and soon I respond as the writer was responding to God's goodness. In times of pressure, instead of turning on your television or going to the refrigerator, take the Word, read aloud one of the Psalms and declare it to be the expression of your own heart to God. It will bring you into liberty and victory.

When Paul the Apostle spoke of singing, he declared, "I will sing with the spirit, and I will sing with the understanding also" (1 Corinthians 14:15). "Singing with the Spirit" refers not only to singing a song inspired by the Spirit but singing in the language of the Spirit. This language of the Spirit has not come as a prayer language only, but also as a praise language. Don't be afraid to release that language melodiously. How I used to thrill hearing our congregation sing in the Spirit, using a variety of languages and rising and falling in pitch as though all knew the song ahead of time. The conscious mind seemed to be bypassed, and the spirit within was unhampered in releasing praise unto the Lord.

It is not unusual for a person given to praise to awaken in the middle of the night aware that the Spirit within him is praising the Lord in song. If our conscious mind did not establish such a rigorous censorship, I would not be surprised if this would occur frequently during the waking hours too.

A third way to perform praise is listed at the end of verse 1 of this 149th Psalm: "And his praise in the congregation of saints." Here it is suggested that spoken, shouted, joyful praise can also be part of our public worship and testimony when we come together. One sometimes cannot help but wonder if much of our assembling is not self-centered or duty motivated. If we came together to "behold Him," would we not involve ourselves in praise far more than we do? If we had a common vision, would there not be more of a common expression?

You will recall how awkward it was to bring our whole congregation into praise. Individuals had learned to praise, our prayer groups did fairly well, but it seemed so strange to do it in the main auditorium. We had found it helpful to take a portion of the service time and invite everyone to leave the pews and gather at the front of the church and down the center aisle. When we were packed together, shoulder to shoulder, I would lead them in vocal, united expressions of praise. There was something about breaking the pattern of sitting in the pew, plus the closeness and even physical contact, that seemed to break down inhibitions and made it easier for the people to be released in praise.

Eventually, we made the transition from having to come to the front for praise to being able to praise standing in the pew rows, and what heavenly music it was to hear such variety in expression, but all praising. We had more than twenty different denominations represented in our congregation, and the differences in heritage and custom made for great variety. I was reminded that the incense used in the Holy of Holies of the tabernacle was compounded from several different fragrances to produce what God desired. How fragrant will be the praises of His people as we stand in His presence in Heaven from every tribe, nation, language, culture, and religious heritage and sing and shout His praises in the eternities! Second Chronicles 29:28 gives us a beautiful picture of a praising people: "And all the congregation worshipped, and the singers sang, and the trumpeters sounded: and all this continued until the burnt offering was finished."

Do you have any concept of how long it might have taken to totally consume a bullock on the grates of the altar, reduce it to ashes, cool the ashes enough that men could take them out with shovels, put them in basins, and carry them outside the camp for burial? I have a suspicion that it took from early morning until late evening, and during this whole time, the congregation praised the Lord!

[For additional Scriptures on congregational praise, see the appendix.]

In verse 2 of the 149th Psalm, a fourth method of praising the Lord is given. "Let Israel rejoice in him that made him." The Hebrew word translated "rejoice," means, literally, "to brighten up." In Psalm 68:3, the word "rejoice" comes from the Hebrew word "to be bright, cheerful, make mirth." To rejoice in the Lord, then, is more than reciting words of praise and adoration; it is a total change of attitude, countenance, and expression.

The Old Testament priest never came into the divine presence until he had stopped by the laver for a fresh look, a cleansing, and a refreshing. We need to learn how to use the "laver of the Word" for "brightening up" on preparation for worship.

We do this regularly in the secular world. Have you ever stepped into a store just in time to overhear the manager angrily disciplining one of his employees, and before you could slip out, you were seen? To your amazement, the manager instantly changed his manner, the tone and inflection of his voice. His face softened, and he even smiled a little as he approached you with a cheery, "May I help you?" For the sake of potential profits, he rapidly exerted his will to brighten up, to become cheerful. To have done otherwise might very well have cost him a customer. He recognized that he had no right to inflict his personal feelings of anger and resentment upon the public.

This matter of "rejoicing in the Lord," is one of learning to be controlled by your will levels instead of your emotional levels. It is learning not to inflict upon the Lord all your angers, bitternesses, and resentments that the frustrations of life have produced in your emotional nature.

Oh, how often our public worship services are ruined because we've never learned to rule our emotions instead of being ruled by them. Our worship is affected by the weather, stock market, physical condition, or home relationships. This should never be allowed. We do not praise as a release of natural emotions; we praise as a release of emotions stirred by seeing that Jesus is Lord in everything. We learn that all things "come to pass" – nothing comes to stay! We learn to respond to God the Father who has accepted the responsibility for our lives whether they are in a good cycle or a bad one.

What does your life, as you are living it now, have to do with the excellence and greatness of God, of His gifts, graces, and benefits? Paul and Silas, in the midst of the dungeon at Philippi, chose to rejoice in the Lord in praise. Happy is the saint who has learned not to base his praise upon his feelings. Discipline yourself to praise the Lord no matter what your circumstances in life may be. God sees this discipline as a form of praise in its own right, and His Word calls it, "a brightening up."

Blessed is the Christian, who, when asked "How are you," does not give an "organ recital" but instead expresses the brightness of the Spirit within him. People do not need to hear your problems; they do need to hear your praises.

The last of Psalm 149:2 suggests still a fifth way to praise the Lord. "Let the children of Zion be joyful in their King." Being joyful, or joy filled, is one of Christ's goals for His people. He told His disciples, "These things have I spoken unto you, that my joy might remain in you, and that your joy might be full" (John 15:11). Peter wrote, "Whom having not seen, ye love; in whom, though now ye see him not, yet believing, ye rejoice with joy unspeakable and full of glory" (1 Pet. 1:8). Jude reminds us, "Now unto him that is able to keep you from falling, and to present you faultless before the presence of his glory with exceeding joy … " (Jude 24).

God has purposed joy for His people. Happiness is dependent upon happenings, but joy is dependent upon Jesus. Jesus brought joy to people wherever He went, and He is still doing it! Those who are seeing Him, hearing Him, and believing Him are being filled with "exceeding joy" and "joy unspeakable and full of glory."

However, it is not the possession of the joy that produces the praise, but the release of that joy. "Make a joyful noise unto the God of Jacob" (Psalm 81:1). Have you ever heard the expression, "Well, I can't sing, but I can make a joyful noise?" The Bible makes no reference to any inability to stay on pitch, but emphasizes that we are to speak out our praises unto the Lord.

We need to recognize that until praise is vocalized, it is not completely expressed. There is a difference between thinking and thanking. We see this in our day-to-day relationships. You may be sincerely grateful for something, but until you express your gratitude to the giver, something is missing, incomplete. Similarly, praise is not just a heart attitude, it is the expression of that attitude. Attitudes of praise should produce expressions of praise. Lift up your voice—lift up your hands—let others know of your appreciation and joy.

Just as the uninhibited child who is filled with the emotions of joy will leap and jump and can hardly be made to sit still, so God knows that reception of His divine joy will produce similar reactions in His joy-filled children.

I am not suggesting that we take our liberty to spin around like a top before the Lord in the downtown cathedral, but wouldn't it be nice to want to? Wouldn't it be proper to give a physical evidence of some kind to the joy God's presence brings to us even if we must restrict it to non-public worship sessions? It is not wrong to let your body demonstrate what your spirit feels, as long as it does not affect the liberty of someone else too adversely.

The sixth method of praise listed in Psalm 149 is, "Let them praise his name in the dance" (v. 3). The International Standard Bible Encyclopedia tells us that dancing in Old Testament times was primarily a leaping, often to musical accompaniment. When we read that "David danced before the Lord with all his might" (2 Sam. 6:14), we have a picture of him leaping higher and higher as he ran before the returning Ark. His joy was unbounded. He had laid aside his kingly robes and wore the simple linen ephod, as a priest before the Lord, and excelled all the priests in his expression of joy that the symbol of the Lord's presence was returning to Jerusalem.

Psalm 150:4 also calls for us to "Praise him with the … dance." Literally it says, "Praise Him by leaping before Him." Why? Perhaps this "leaping" has best been explained by David in Psalm 30:11-12: "Thou hast turned for me my mourning into dancing: thou hast put off my sackcloth, and girded me with gladness; To the end that my glory may sing praise to thee, and not be silent. O Lord my God, I will give thanks unto thee for ever." David's leaping and dancing before the Lord was simply a physical demonstration of the great change God had effected in him. It was an expression of the emotion of gladness, and he saw it as a method of giving thanks unto the Lord.

Perhaps the greatest point of resistance in praise is in allowing one's body to become involved in responding to the Lord. Repeatedly I have seen people become angry at even the suggestion that they lift their hands before the Lord, much less dance before Him. I've spent many hours counseling with people who "just couldn't see the sense in raising hands as part of worship," yet without exception when they finally overcame their rebellion and raised their hands, they broke into beautiful beginning praise.

At a conference in Florida recently, a woman reported to me that she had broken into praise the previous day because, for the first time in her life, she had been able to raise her hands in public. When I congratulated her for such an exercise of will, she said it was not due to her will, but because her husband had reached over, taken her hands, and jerked them up into the air. Nonetheless, it brought her the desired release.

There is something about getting the body involved that brings an inner release. I suppose there is something in our pride that does not want to "make a spectacle of ourselves." We have not yet learned to release ourselves fully in the presence of the Lord. We get physically involved in releasing our emotions at sporting events, but feel it is beneath our precious dignity to do so in church. We are urged, nevertheless, to lift our hands (Psalm 63:4); clap our hands (Psalm 47:1); stand before the Lord (Psalm 135:2); bow down before the Lord and kneel before Him (Psalm 95:6); and dance, or leap, before the Lord (Psalm 149:3).

Finally, this 149th Psalm suggests, in verse 3, "Let them sing praises unto him with the timbrel and harp." Playing instruments in connection with praise and worship is mentioned at least sixteen times in the Old Testament and four times in the New. Although some other species of God's creation can make limited musical intonations, man is the only one of God's creatures that can make a mechanical contrivance and then play music on it. Man is not only creative and artistic, but he has a soul that cries out for expression in various forms of music including instrumentation. Psalm 150 lists every class of musical instrument known in that day and says, "Praise Him with these."

Israel used the trumpet to sound the alarm, to rally her armies, and to call the people to worship. Psalm 81:3 refers to the call throughout the land to return to Jerusalem for one of the three required feast days: "Blow up the trumpet in the new moon, in the time appointed, on our solemn feast day." The keynote of the feasts was joy and praise.

Often we feel that praise must be a private thing, yet as we have seen, the Scripture clearly teaches us that praise should also be a public expression. The purpose for our coming together is worship, and praise is a vital part of that worship.

Let Psalm 149 be your handbook on beginning to praise. First, get involved personally, "Praise ye the Lord." Second, "Sing unto God." Third, unite in congregational praise. Fourth, learn to "brighten up" when coming into His Presence. Fifth, we need to allow ourselves to be "joyful" and to release our emotions Godward. Sixth, we can praise the Lord in the dance. Allow your body some participation in worship. And seventh, play whatever instrument you can as a praise before the Lord.

Recently I was a speaker at a large youth gathering in a major Canadian city. I was startled to see a young man, in his mid-twenties, stand up on the platform with two tiny bells in his hands. As we sang, he played those two tiny bells, and with over 2,000 people singing, several guitars being amplified, and a hugh pipe organ blasting forth, I doubt if he was heard even in the front row. But as I watched his face, I realized he wasn't playing to be heard; he was praising the Lord on those two bells, and he was lost in his praise.

You need not do great things to become a praiser, you need

only do something! Praise is neither thought or feeling, it is expression! It should not be governed by emotion, it should be a releasing of the emotion. Praise begins in the spirit of man, is governed by the will of man, and in its expression uses the whole of man.

Praise ye the Lord.

8

Persuasions to Praise

As a teenage preacher, I did not get involved very much in dating girls and was quite sure that I would never marry. But about the second month I was in Bible college, I noticed a young lady who had arrived late in the fall term. Before long, she was assigned as the pianist to the ministry team in which I was the preacher. There was something different about this girl. Just being with her persuaded me to drastically reappraise my stand on dating. Before the school year was over, I had been so persuaded by her company that I proposed marriage to her, and on June 20, 1943, Judson "the woman-hater" became Judson the married man. Oh, the power of persuasion!

Twenty-six times the New Testament uses some form of the word "persuade." Perhaps the two most familiar instances are: "For I know whom I have believed, and am persuaded that he is able to keep that which I have committed unto him against that day" (2 Timothy 1:12); and "For I am persuaded, that neither death, nor life, nor angels, nor principalities, nor powers, nor things present, nor things to come, Nor height, nor depth, nor any other creature, shall be able to separate us from the love of God, which is in Christ Jesus our Lord" (Romans 8:38-39).

Saul the persecutor became Paul the persuaded! Something happened that caused him to reverse his viewpoint.

This is the way the Lord brings us into praise. He does not use force, but He does present facts. He is far less commanding in this matter of praise than He is conciliatory. He does not want to make us praise Him, He wants to motivate us into praise. Unless there is an inner desire that is responding to divine stimuli, our praise would be no more pleasing to God than the "thank you" of a child who had been threatened with punishment if he did not say those words of appreciation. An old song we used to sing included the words, "He would not force them against their will, He just made them willing to go." How illustrative this is of God's methods of bringing us into praise and worship. He persuades us!

In the first seven verses of the 149th Psalm there are at least seven motivations for praise listed, seven persuaders God uses to move us to respond to Him in praise.

The first persuasion is to praise God for who He is! "Praise ye the Lord" (v. 1). Until we get a glimpse of who He is, we'll never be good praisers. We must see Him as gracious; we must see Him as merciful; we must see Him as plenteous in love and full of compassion. We must see Him as He is revealed in His Word, not as He is expressed in religion.

When God began to lead our church in Oregon into praise, it didn't take us two years to learn to raise our hands or say "Hallelujah" and "Praise the Lord." But it took us two years to come into a praise that was a real release of what was within us. We found it necessary to re-evaluate the Lord in our concepts before we could fully praise Him. Because of our religious heritage, some of us were bound in legalism. Our concept of God was the concept of an officer of the law, observing us with an eye to our failures, and it's hard to praise that kind of a God.

Others, because of their background, had such a high and

lofty concept of God that they considered Him unapproachable. They couldn't imagine His being involved with us personally. Trying to come into His presence with praise was akin to seeking an audience with the president of the United States or with the queen of England. But slowly the Holy Spirit re-guided us through the Bible to see that the Word makes God very available and deeply related to us. He is revealed as "Father," "Brother," "Husband," "Bridegroom," enabling us to respond to Him on a comfortable level.

When my wife and I were ministering in Indonesia at a minister's institute, we were told not to expect much in the way of emotional response. Because of the extremely crowded living conditions on the island of Java and the depth to which they were rooted in their ancient culture, emotional response had been greatly repressed. In this conference we had about 350 pastors representing some twenty-eight different denominations and foundations, which was quite a cross-section of religion for Indonesia.

All we did was lift up Jesus as we taught the Word. We were not preaching on praise or worship; we taught on the call of God to Moses. But when these brethren began to see what David had seen, they also began to feel what David had felt—and to do what David had done. Without instruction or urging, they began to weep, shout, clap their hands, praise, and on one occasion, even marched around the building rejoicing in the Lord. As their concept of God was lifted to a fresh orientation, their response was spontaneous and free. They praised because they saw the person of God. They got involved with the divine presence.

One of the finest and strongest motivations to praise is simply seeing Him as He is presented in the Word. As we lift up Jesus anew and see Him as loving and gentle, as the total provision for our needs in this life as well as King, there will be a response of praise unto the Lord, because love must find an expression, and praise is a natural response of love. We praise Him, first of all, for who He is.

Secondly, we praise Him for what He has done. "Let Israel rejoice in him that made him" (Psalm 149:2). Over in Isaiah 43:1 we read, "Now thus saith the Lord that created thee, O Jacob, and he that formed thee, O Israel, Fear not: for I have redeemed thee, I have called thee by thy name; thou art mine." He has created us; He has formed us; He has redeemed us; He has called us, and He has accepted a father's responsibility over us. This should evoke praise responses within us. Some of us have needlessly created problems for ourselves that have hindered praising. A problem that I had for many years, going way back to my boyhood days, was that I did not like my physical build. My father was the runt of his family, being only six feet, one inch, tall. When my brothers came along, they out-distanced dad by several inches. There was a tradition in our home that when one of us boys passed the height of dad, he got a free milkshake, which, in the depth of the Depression, was a great reward. Well, after many years of "struggle," I finally passed the height of my mother and got an ice cream cone. My brothers are tall, well-built, athletic men, but by stretching my frame to its maximum height, I reach barely five feet nine inches.

For years I carried a tremendous sense of inferiority when I was around my brothers. They made the football team; I made cheerleader. They possessed all the qualities considered "manly," while I was interested in music and books.

But one day, as I was reading Isaiah 43:1, the Holy Spirit said, "Judson, I made you short and gentle."

Previously, I had figured that since I was the first child in the family, God had seen His mistake and corrected it on my brothers. But as I meditated on that verse, my inner bitterness and resentment began to fade. He had made me exactly as I am.

As this truth began to overwhelm me, He spoke further:

"My son, I not only made you, I re-made you. I not only formed you in the womb of your mother, I have also formed you in the womb of the Spirit, and I have re-created you so that you are becoming what I chose you to be from the foundations of the Earth."

You will never know the new realm of praise this released within me. God made me, and He re-made me. He formed me, and He re-formed me. He created me, and He re-created me. He caused me to be born and to be born again.

I believe that you are what you are because of a pattern God has chosen for your life, as well as the choices you have made in your life. But even though your choices haven't been wise, He is nonetheless able to overrule them and bring them into His wisdom, and this should bring forth praise. Don't condemn yourself because you have a Catholic heritage, or Lutheran, or Presbyterian. I had to stop condemning myself because I had a Pentecostal heritage. It isn't what we were, it's what we are becoming that is of concern to God.

In spite of our background, he is bringing us into His foreground, and by a process of melting, molding, and shaping, He is forming us into His own image, making us accepted in the beloved, and causing us to be seated with Him in the heavenlies. And that should produce a praise within our hearts that demands an expression through our mouths. (What I was never able to effect within me, He is able to perfect in me through the operation of His Spirit, so I just stand back and rejoice and praise the Lord that He is doing what I could not do.)

A third persuasion to praise is also given in this second verse: "Let the children of Zion be joyful in their King." How important it is to learn to direct our emotions, for if we do not direct them, they will direct us, and what a miserable life it is to be directed from the emotional level. Obviously, we have only one set of emotions, and these must be used by our spirit and our soul, as well as God's Spirit. Unless there is some means of discharging these emotions safely, they will become overloaded and potentially dangerous. There is nothing more prone to danger than a group of people who are emotionally charged. This forms the basis for all sorts of mob actions. Somehow it causes people to lose sensibility. If overcharged emotionally, we tend to respond to further stimulus without rational consideration. Praise is a God-given, scripturally taught channel of release for the emotions. It enables us to release pent-up feelings in a safe, positive fashion that blesses God and builds us up.

It seems unfair, and potentially unsafe, to build high levels of emotional feeling in our worship service through singing, exhortation, and preaching of the Word if we are not going to give worshipers an opportunity to discharge those emotions. Praise is the divinely appointed manner of release. One of the charges assessed against services with an emotional content is that they tend to produce looseness of behavior among the people. The charge is worth looking at seriously. If the worship service tends to charge people emotionally, and we offer no united way of discharging the emotions, we can expect emotional actions and reactions among the people as they meet socially afterwards. Deep stirrings of love are easily transferred from one person to another. The feeling of joy easily finds as its object something other than that which produced the joy.

It is not too uncommon for people to transfer religious feelings to physical feelings, and nothing delights Satan more. As an answer to this danger, some have felt it safest not to arouse emotions in their religious ritual. Yet Oswald Smith wisely observed, "If you take emotion out of religion, you'll have no motion." The answer is not to restrict the emotion but to release it! Let the saints "be joyful in their King." Learn to release your inner feelings in praise and adoration of God. Let Him benefit from what He has produced within you. If He has stirred you to love, let your love responses be toward Him. If

He has stirred you to the deepest love and appreciation you have ever felt, release it back to Him. He desires it and warmly receives it, and in the process of releasing it, you have spent your emotions and leave them clear for stimuli from other sources.

In my earlier days of pastoring, I used to wind myself to a high emotional pitch each Sunday. I would pray late on Saturday night, rise early Sunday morning for prayer, teach a class in Sunday school, and preach twice on Sunday after conducting the preliminaries of the worship services. By Sunday night, I was so keyed up, I couldn't relax enough to go to sleep, so in pre-television days, I would read until two in the morning, when exhaustion overtook the nervous tension. In later years, I did it the easier way by watching TV until exhaustion overwhelmed me. Usually my Sunday would be followed by a "blue Monday," and it would often take all of Tuesday to bring me out of the slump, for all emotional highs will have equally emotional lows, if we allow them to rule us instead of ruling them.

When I began to move into praise, I learned that the thing that had been wrong was simply that I had not learned to discharge my emotions so that I could relax and sleep. So I learned to release this pent-up emotion unto Him in praise— in song, in clapping my hands, in leaping before the Lord, or whatever avenue of worship seemed most appropriate at the moment. Delightfully, I learned that this not only released me emotionally so I could relax, but it was accepted by the Lord as love and praise. Now when I get all keyed up and can't sleep, I just have a praise session and release all the emotions Godward. It is a good thing to express your emotions to God, and praise is the finest expression that the Scripture has given to us.

A fourth motivation to praise God is given in verse 4 of Psalm 149. "For the Lord taketh pleasure in his people." In His people. When we read, with our limited understanding, the Scriptures concerning the heavens, we tend to feel God must get great pleasure out of all of that. We read of His angels, His glory, His grandeur, His beauty, His throne, and His dominion and power, and we say, "That must give great pleasure to God." Then we read of His creation and again feel this must give great satisfaction to God. We are ourselves so overwhelmed with the creation of God that we have spent billions of dollars to send a few men to the moon just to pick up some rock samples.

But the Scriptures speak of the creation as simply "God's handiwork" (Psalm 19:1). The Hebrew word used here means "needlework, such as crochet or tatting." The entire stellar system that stirs our deepest imaginations is little more than God's hobby expression—just something He did with His hands in a little spare time.

The Scripture says, however, that He takes pleasure in His people. We are the object of the pleasure of God. (We dealt with this in chapter two when considering the god-ward side of the purpose of praise.) God's program is to take pleasure in His people, to be completed in His people, to be satisfied in His people. Man is His glory.

When you genuinely love a person, you are constantly looking for some little way to please them. You listen for every hint or suggestion, because you know a birthday or Christmas is coming. We don't want to ask them outright, nor do we want to miss pleasing them. If we do catch a word, a hint, a suggestion, we hide it in our heart until we can fulfill that expressed desire. God has suggested that praise is the finest gift you can give Him.

Why? When God says, "This gives me pleasure," don't wait until you are mature enough in your relationship to understand why, for you will never mature in that relationship until you obey Him without having to understand the whys. The fact that He says He likes it should be sufficient motivation for you to do it.

Some years ago, as we were becoming aware of this truth

in our church, my sister, under the inspiration of the Spirit, wrote an entire Christmas cantata with praise as its theme. The chorus woven into the cantata repeatedly was, "Sing praise to the Christ of Christmas." It shocked people the first time it was presented, for few had thought of actually praising on Christmas. The second reaction, however, was to take another look at it. We used the cantata repeatedly, for it seemed more appropriate to praise on Christmas than to do anything else. Jesus doesn't need the gold, and frankincense, and the myrrh, but He is obviously pleased with our praise. Psalm 103:21 declares, "Bless ye the Lord...ye ministers of his, that do his pleasure." It is in the blessing of the Lord, in praising Him, that we are giving pleasure unto God.

A fifth motivating persuasion to praise is seen in Psalm 149:4: "The Lord...will beautify the meek with salvation." We are, moved to praise Him when we see what we've become! Please stop saying, "No good thing dwelleth in me," for God dwells within you. He is putting His Spirit within, with all of His glory and beauty. Even the most homely of us have been beautified with the workings of God. As you read the Song of Solomon, you will note that again and again he describes the beauty of the girl. It is a conferred beauty, it is a divine beauty, it is a glorious beauty—but it has become her beauty!

Some years ago, the Lord spoke to me and said He felt it was time for me to see my inner self as He saw it. I pleaded with Him not to give me such a revelation at that time. I felt it would completely devastate me. I was headed to South America for ministry and was fearful and full of self-doubts already. However, He was most insistent that day, and more against my will than with the cooperation of that will, the Lord began to describe me.

I will never forget the experience! For more than an hour the Lord spoke of the way the Godhead saw me. He described ministries I have not yet come into. He spoke of inner qualities

I know I do not now possess. He described my motivations as He saw them, my mannerisms, my methods, and my ministries. After a lengthy period of hearing, I interrupted the flow of the Spirit by protesting that this certainly was not a description of me. He must have someone else in mind, for the picture He had painted bore very little resemblance to the Judson Cornwall I had lived with for nearly half a century.

His reply to my protest was, "My son, I have been describing you as We see you, for We are looking at the blueprints of your life. As a master architect sees the building completed when he is looking at the drawings, so We see the finished product from the beginning. As you see yourself, you are only an excavated hole in the ground with footings poured and some steel reinforcing in place. Everything around you seems to be in disarray. But We see you as complete in Christ and have described what you shall be in Him." Hallelujah!

When Jesus comes for His Church, He is not coming for a worn-out, beaten-down, decrepit, aging bride that He has to sneak out in the dark of the night because of shame. The Scripture says He is going to come for a Church that is glorious—without spot, or wrinkle, or blemish, or any such thing. Does that fit your present observation of the Church? How, then, can the necessary change be effected? He is cleansing the Church, changing the Church, and conferring His beauty upon her. He will present the bride unto himself in the form He desires her to be. As she praises Him, He changes her. What a persuasion to praise! Every look into a mirror should motivate us to further praising of the Lord.

The next major persuasion to praise given in Psalm 149 is that it brings us into God's presence. Verse 1 speaks of praising "in the congregation of saints," while verse 6 speaks of letting "the high praises of God be in their mouth." When Ken Taylor translated Ephesians 3:15 in The Living Bible, he wrote, "I … pray to the Father of all the great family of God—some of them already in heaven and some down here on earth ..."

How short-sighted most of us are in believing that the true Church of God is totally here on Earth, some of us even believing that it is in the walls of our denomination or even our local church. God's Church is far greater than anything on Earth right now. It is composed of saints of all the ages, some of whom have already gone on to their reward in the presence of the Lord, and others now living and representing Christ on the Earth. Some are worshiping God on Earth, the rest are worshiping God in Heaven. But all are praising.

In Hebrews 12:22-24 we read that we, the living and earth-bound, "are come unto" nine "things:" "But ye are come unto mount Sion, and unto the city of the living God, the heavenly Jerusalem, and to an innumerable company of angels, To the general assembly and church of the firstborn, which are written in heaven, and to God the Judge of all, and to the spirits of just men made perfect, and to Jesus the mediator of the new covenant, and to the blood of sprinkling, that speaketh better things than that of Abel." All these things are in the heavenlies.

As we looked at Isaiah 6:1-4 and Revelation 19:1-7, we saw everything praising and worshiping the Lord! Praise seems to be the main occupation on high. Praises on high, or "high praises."

When Psalm 149 calls us to join the "congregation of saints" and to enter with "the high praises of God ... in their mouths," I believe it is saying that there are times when the Church on Earth rises in her praise levels to join the praise level of the Church in Heaven. All our praising is imperfect, but that part of the Church that has already entered into the heavenlies has, by now, learned a far more perfect form of praise. They have "seen Him as He is" and are motivated by spiritual vision, not earthly and carnal reasonings. When we can join our praise with their praise, we enter into a much higher realm of praise. We have already mentioned that Psalm 22:3 states that God "inhabitest the praises of Israel." Here, however, we see that not only does God come down to join us in our praising, but there are times when our praising elevates us into the spiritual heavenlies, and as Paul, we find ourselves "caught up to the third heaven" (2 Corinthians 12:2).

To transcend time and space and enter into that "other world" that is entirely spiritual is a desire deep in the heart of almost everyone, although often so repressed as to be hidden even from the individual. In fact, it is this repressed craving that gives rise to the occult and witchcraft. Man wants to break the barrier of his small world. God has offered us a "time-space machine" that enables us to enter into His world and presence. He calls it high praises. Shouldn't this persuade you to become a praiser of the Lord?

The seventh persuading motivation to praise in this Psalm is that praise becomes the key weapon in our battle against Satan, verse 7. But since this is at the heart of the next chapter "The Power of Praise," we will not discuss it now beyond saying that rebuking Satan was beyond even the scope of authority given Michael, who was of equal rank with Lucifer in the heavenlies. Praise is our greatest weapon against the Satanic!

Are these motivations sufficient to cause you to magnify the Lord? Lift up your voice and praise the Lord. Praise Him for who He is. Praise Him for what He has done. Praise Him to release your emotions of joy. Praise Him to give Him pleasure. Praise Him for the beauty He is producing in you. Praise Him to enter into His presence. Just praise Him.

9

The Power of Praise

"Why boastest thou thyself in mischief, O mighty man?...God shall likewise destroy thee for ever ... I will praise thee for ever, because thou hast done it" (Psalm 52:1, 5, 9).

The 149th Psalm, that has given us some guidelines in the performance of praise and has gently sought to persuade us to praise, also teaches us that there is tremendous power in praise. God has not left us defenseless, He has given us mighty spiritual weapons, and praise is chief among them.

In Psalm 149:7-9, there are five specific functions of praise that illustrate to us the greatness, the magnitude, the loftiness, and the power of praise, when it is used as a weapon. First, it says we can "execute vengeance upon the heathen" (v. 7). Secondly, it declares that we can execute "punishments upon the people" (v. 7). Third, praise is "to bind their kings with chains" (v. 8), and fourth, "to bind ... their nobles with fetters of iron" (v. 8). The fifth function of praise is "to execute upon them the judgment written" (v. 9).

Praise is immensely powerful! It is eternally effective! It

enables us to deal directly in the spirit world. It allows us to come to grips with rebellious men and demonic forces and gain the victory over them. All with praise—high praise!

In seeking to understand this, let's define the enemies listed here, then seek to understand the weapon offered, and finally see if we can comprehend the nature of the conflict. As to the nature of the enemy, there are two classes of men mentioned and two categories in the spirit world. The men are called "heathen" and "the people." The expression "heathen" in the Old Testament consistently refers to those who are without God—those who have no knowledge of God, no acceptance of Him, and no relationship to Him. There is to be an execution of vengeance upon them.

"The people," in contrast to "the heathen" in verse 7, most likely refers to God's covenant people who were often called "the Lord's people" or simply "the people." These are not to know God's vengeance, only punishment from God. God deals with the heathen one way, and with His people another. The Scriptures declare, "For whom the Lord loveth he chasteneth, and scourgeth every son whom he receiveth" (Hebrews 12:6). Also, "But when we are judged, we are chastened of the Lord, that we should not be condemned with the world" (1 Corinthians 11:32).

The two categories of the spirit world mentioned are "their kings" and "their nobles" (v. 8). The king of the heathen is Satan. He is considered the god of this age. Jesus himself referred to him as "the prince of this world" (John 14:30; 16:11), and Paul called him "the prince of the power of the air" (Ephesians 2:2). If their king is Satan, then their nobles would be the lesser powers in the Satanic realm. Ephesians 6:11-12 lists the Satanic kingdom's five levels of authority: "Put on the whole armour of God, that ye may be able to stand against the wiles of [1] the devil. For we wrestle not against flesh and blood, but against [2] principalities, against [3] powers, against [4] the rulers of the darkness of this world, against [5] spiritual wickedness in high places."

While it is not in the scope of this book to try to fully define each of these levels, we are aware that Satan's kingdom is patterned after God's Kingdom and has decreasing levels of power from Satan, through the other fallen angels, to the demons (evil spirits). (See "Demons" in the appendix.)

All are under the control of Satan their king as Revelation 16:13-14 affirms: "And I saw, issuing from the mouth of the dragon [a New Testament name for Satan] ... three foul spirits like frogs; for they are demonic spirits, performing signs, who go abroad to the kings of the whole world" (RSV).

Also, remember that the Jews charged Jesus with casting out demons through Beelzebub the chief of the devils (Luke 11:15). Strong, in his Greek dictionary, (appended to his complete concordance) affirms that "Beelzebub" is a name of Satan. Satan, in Christ's time, was recognized as chief of the devils. The demons are certainly not "free agents;" they issue from Satan's mouth and are under his headship as Beelzebub.

There is a noticeable progression in this listing of the enemies in Ephesians 6:11-12. From the heathen, who are quite non-threatening to most of us; to "the people" to whom we are far more vulnerable because of the fellowship of love; to Satan, with whom few of us will ever have a direct confrontation; to the progressively depreciating power of his kingdom, against which we probably struggle more than against all the others put together. Yet, we are taught that praise is a weapon against them all.

We need to look at this weapon called "high praises." There are degrees of praise, just as there are degrees of anointing. We usually start praising in the lower levels of faith and anointing, often getting involved first in the realm of the soulish, the emotions, and then moving into the realm of the mind, the will, and finally through our spirit, into His Spirit. When we begin to release God's Spirit through using praise, we are reaching a higher realm of praise.

The praise spoken of here as being a weapon against the enemies of the Kingdom of God is called, specifically, "high praises of God." This refers to the praises being offered on high: "Let the saints be joyful in glory [in Heaven]: let them sing aloud upon their beds [on Earth]" (Psalm 149:5).

We are not yet made perfect. We are still greatly limited in our perception of spiritual things. We are not aware of being surrounded by an innumerable company of angels, although the Scripture teaches us that we are. Yet there are times when we begin to soar in the Spirit, and are allowed of God to enter into the praise of the full Church of Christ. The segment that we belong to here joins the praise of the segment that is up there. The main activity of the Church that has gone on is worship and praise, and they have come into perfection in this because they behold the face of the One they are praising. They have come into an understanding of justice. They've come into an understanding of vengeance. They now comprehend the true Lordship of Christ over the Earth. They see into the purposes of God. They can praise better and higher because they can see what we cannot see.

We're performing in faith; they're performing in fact. We're functioning in flesh; they're functioning in spirit. They have been taught by the angels; we have been taught of man. We are very limited; they are unlimited. Were it not for the common bond of the blood of Christ and the love of God, there might very well never be anything analogous between these groups. Yet Hebrews 12:1 speaks of the heavenly group being "a cloud of witnesses," cheering the earthly group on in the race of life.

At times God allows us, in our praises, to rise above our emotional levels, and even above our faith level, and join praises with the heavenly forces. Often, when this happens, we are not consciously aware that we have joined praises with angels and the spirits of just men made perfect. But just as surely as there was a joining of Jesus with Moses and Elijah on the Mount of Transfiguration, so, I believe, there are times of joining of the Saints on Earth with the Saints in glory, in responses of praise that enable us to let the high praises of God be in our mouth. When we get so joined and involved, when the saints are in communion, if you like, our praise is purer, stronger, and more properly directed—even though we may be saying the same words we've always said. And there comes a new direction, a new flow, a new depth of faith, a fresh authority in our praise.

It is interesting that where our translation says these high praises are to be in our "mouth," the literal Hebrew is "in their throats." Just as Jesus did not say it would be out of the brain but out of the belly that rivers of living water should flow (John 7:38), so here it does not say the high praises would be in the mind but in the throat. As surely as tongues go beyond the conscious level (supraconscious), so some praises go beyond the mental level of the conscious mind and are the result of direct inspiration of the Holy Spirit. It is as though the Spirit himself is doing the praising. It may be in tongues, yet is more likely to be in your own language. But your intellect is not feeding your vocal chords, the Holy Spirit is directing the expression of praise. He is taking the heavenly "high praises" and flowing them into your mouth. When this happens, you are not just dealing with praise as an expression, you're dealing with praise as a weapon, and what a fabulous weapon praise is!

"Let the high praises of God be in their mouth, and a two-edged sword in their hand" (Psalm 149:6). Never reverse God's prescribed order. The praise is to be in the mouth, not the sword. The first chapter of Revelation shows the sword in the mouth of Christ, but nowhere does the Scripture put the sword in the mouth of the saints. It belongs in their hand. Ephesians 6:17 calls this, "the sword of the Spirit, which is the word of God." When we try to battle with the sword in our mouth, we only wound, divide, and slay. How the Body of Christ has been hurt by indiscriminate quoting of Scripture one to another as "proof texts" or "Scripture clubs," to force or coerce another to our viewpoint. It's not the quoting of Scripture that is going to bring us into victory, but the release of the high praises of God through our mouth!

Yes, we need the Scriptures, but keep them in the hand. What we really need is the combination of the Spirit and the Word, praises based upon the promises, spoken words flowing from the written Word, responses Godward based upon revelations manward from the Word.

Now that we've seen the enemies, and something of the weapon God has given us to use against these enemies, let's seek to understand the nature of the conflict and how to use our weapon of praise.

The 149th Psalm says our weapon can successfully "execute vengeance upon the heathen, and punishments upon the people; ... bind their kings with chains, and their nobles with fetters of iron; ... execute upon them the judgment written" (v. 7-9).

It is difficult for some to see God as both a God of love and a God of judgment. The concept of using praise to bring vengeance, punishment, binding, and judgment upon others causes some people to cringe. They declare that this is not New Testament at all, that this isn't the God that they know. But it really is the New Testament and the God that you should know!

In Revelation 6:10 we hear the voice of the martyrs crying, "How long, O Lord, holy and true, dost thou not judge and avenge our blood on them that dwell on the earth?" and in Revelation 11:17-18 we hear the twenty-four elders worshiping God saying, "We give thee thanks, O Lord God Almighty ... because thou hast taken to thee thy great power, and hast reigned. And the nations were angry, and thy wrath is come. .

.and shouldest destroy them which destroy the earth."

God declares in His Word, "Vengeance is mine; I will repay, saith the Lord" (Romans 12:19). God doesn't want you to have a vengeful spirit, because He knows it will destroy you. Man is not strong enough to handle vengeance, so Jesus said, "Love your enemies, do good to them which hate you, Bless them that curse you, and pray for them which despitefully use you" (Luke 6:27-28).

God simply says, "I'm strong enough to hold this in remembrance, and if they will not submit to the love that is flowing through you, vengeance is Mine. I'll take care of it for you."

When I read, in the church history books, of the thousands who have been slain by the heathen; or review Fox's Book of Martyrs and see the inhumanities of man to man because of his testimony of God; and when I see, in my ministry to pastors throughout the world, what people—Christian people—have done to some of God's servants, something inside me cries out, "Oh, God, don't forget Your promise that vengeance is Yours! Don't forget to repay them!" It is not because I am harsh or hard-hearted; I am, in reality, quite soft-hearted. But I cannot handle seeing people destroyed by other people, and continue to love the destroyers, unless I know that God is a just God as well as a justifier. I must be aware that God ultimately will pour out His vengeance upon those who reject His love. Since I know that vengeance is His, and the punishments are written, I can continue to love—because that is the only hope of yet reaching them for Christ.

Our position is not to plead for vengeance or judgment, we are to let the high praises of God be in our mouth. We can praise God, when normally we would be calling for vengeance, because we know God is a just God. And we know that He will take care of it His way.

Some years ago, on a Sunday morning in our church, we were moved into a very high level of praise. It flowed like a river, and continued to lift us higher and still higher into realms of praise, greater than we had ever experienced before. We could see no visible results among us, but there was a sense of understanding that God was doing something very extraordinary. That afternoon I received a phone call from a young man who had gone out from our congregation to pastor a church less than two hundred miles from us. He asked what had been happening in the church about 11:15 that morning. I told him of the beautiful high level of praise we had reached, and asked him why he had asked about it. He explained that at 11:15 one of his deacons stood to his feet in the midst of the meeting and began walking down the center aisle of the church with anger in his eyes. As the treasurer of the church and its most moneyed member, he had for years assumed the leadership in matters of policy and managed to have his own way. Before the entire congregation he said, "Pastor, I demand your resignation. I'm sick and tired of this emphasis on praise and your constant calls to prayer."

I was familiar with the history of that church, and knew that deacon had successfully demanded and received the resignation of other pastors. This young pastor did not know what to do. He looked at the deacon, looked at his own wife, and began to quake with an inner fear. The deacon advanced further and repeated his demand for a resignation. When he got to about the second row of pews he suddenly stopped, his eyes opened wide as though he saw something, and he turned white with fear. He reached into his pocket, pulled out pen and paper, and began to write a note. He handed it to the pastor behind the pulpit and hastily walked out the front door of the church. The note was his resignation as deacon.

As soon as the man left the church, the glory of the Lord filled the building, and the congregation came into a beautiful level of praise and worship, and people began to make things right one with another. The pastor still had not made any movement; he was dumbfounded. During the time of praise and worship, he asked the Lord what had happened. The Lord told him that the home church had gone into high praises which enabled God himself to deal with the rebel directly. "[With] the high praises of God ... in their mouth ... [they] execute punishments upon the people."

This, however, is not the end of the story. Some time later, I received a letter from a South American country where a young man from our congregation was laboring. He asked what had happened on that very same Sunday. Then he told me that three of the town officials had determined to close their church, using some technicality of a previous violation of building codes in the construction of the building. The word had gone out that anyone who attended the church would be arrested, and not many people were taking a chance on that. At the time our congregation was in praise, this young man went to his late afternoon service, which they had instead of an evening service, only to find an empty building. He went in, picked up his accordion, and began to have a one-man song service. The blessing of the Lord began to fill his soul, so he had a testimony service—both leading and participating in it. He then felt led to go ahead and preach the message he had prepared for his people, even to giving an altar call, as usual. To his utter amazement, two members of the city council walked through the doors of the church and came to the altar. These men had been standing outside, watching through the window, having come to arrest anyone attending the services. They were so over-awed at the sight of a preacher conducting a service with nobody there, that they had remained to watch. The Lord came in His convicting power upon them, and they were persuaded to answer His call. As a result, the church now has the official blessing of the city. They have had to enlarge the building twice since then. The praising of one congregation reached out many thousands of miles and did the impossible.

Praise not only works as a foil for men, whether heathen or Christians, it is also a most effective weapon against the evil-spirit world. This passage promises that with "the high praises of God ... in their mouth ... [they] bind their kings with chains, and their nobles with fetters of iron." We've already determined that this is the Satanic kingdom. Jesus clearly stated that we are not going to be successful in taking out of the strong man's house that which we think is ours, unless we first bind the strong man (Mark 3:27). The time has come for the Church of Jesus Christ to come back to the position where we bind the strong man with chains and his lesser emissaries with fetters of iron: then we can go in and totally spoil him of everything that he has taken from the Church.

The Church needs the faith that we let the enemy take away from us. We need the ministries that we have let the enemy steal. We need our children back, our love returned, our authorities in the Word restored. We can have them, if we will bind the "strong man" with "chains and fetters of iron." It is when we come into the high praises of God that God will bind the Satanic, put bondages upon it, put limitations on it, so that you and I have true deliverance and freedom. It is done with praise, not pleading. God wants His people to learn the lesson that if we will praise God with the high praises, He'll take care of any Satanic and demonic forces that are around, and bring forth a binding upon them, instead of letting them bring forth a binding upon us.

With the high praises of God in our mouth, balanced with the two-edged sword in our hand, we bind, put in chains, execute vengeance, bring forth divine victory, transcend the miles, and bring unto God that which He has determined—"the judgment written"—whether deliverance or destruction.

Second Corinthians 10:3-5 tells us something about our weapons: "We do not war after the flesh: (For the weapons of our warfare are not carnal, but mighty through God to the pulling down of strong holds;) Casting down imaginations, and every high thing that exalteth itself against the knowledge of God, and bringing into captivity every thought to the obedience of Christ."

This passage was made very much alive to me some years ago. God was moving our church into a more vital relationship with Him through worship and praise, and one of the men of my board was very much against this moving. He and I had been good friends, but he now felt that I was absolutely wrong, and no amount of my seeking to communicate my vision could reach him. Levels of immaturity in me matched the levels of immaturity in him, and between the two of us, there arose a clash.

This man was a man of power, and he used his power against me. We were in a building program at the time, and he was the only man in my congregation who really understood construction. At one board meeting he declared, "Either Cornwall resigns as pastor and gets out, or I resign as being in charge of the building program, and I get out." After prayer, there was a short delay; then he took the key to the church out of his pocket and spoke directly to me. "Either your key is on the floor in ten seconds or mine is." I called what I thought was a bluff and found he was not bluffing. He threw his key down and that was that.

For months we were at opposite poles from each other. I felt I had done everything that could be done. I had pled with him, prayed for him, and finally, in my mind, written him off as hopeless. Then I began to read Ken Taylor's paraphrase, The Living Letters, and found he had translated the above passage in this way: "It is true that I am an ordinary, weak human being, but I don't use human plans and methods to win my battles. I use God's mighty weapons, not those made by men, to knock down the devil's strongholds. These weapons can break down every proud argument against God and every wall that can be built to keep men from finding him. With these weapons I can capture rebels and bring them back to God, and change them into men whose hearts' desire is obedience to Christ. I will use these weapons against every rebel who remains after I have first used them on you yourselves, and you surrender to Christ."

God spoke to me, telling me that here was the solution to my longstanding problem. But I could not see it until He finally said, "My son, if you will use My weapon, you can drag that man back to captivity—to a man whose heart's desire is to serve Me. You can win him to Me, and to yourself, if you use My weapon. Praise Me for this man."

For a while, this was beyond my comprehension. But after finding no encouragement from other members of my staff, who, with me, had written this brother off as hopeless, I tried reading the verses aloud and said, "Lord, I praise You for this man and for everything he has done to me. And I praise You for this verse."

At first, the response on my part was very empty, but again God spoke. "If you can break through to genuinely praise Me for what that man has done and for what that man means to Me, I will make that verse come to pass in his life."

I praised for six hours—without success. I paused in the praising only long enough to minister in the evening service, then, sending my wife home alone, stayed in the office praising until the early hours of the morning. Finally God sparked faith to believe what I had been saying all those long hours. I was able to say with real genuineness, "I thank You, I praise You, I praise You for these two years. They have been glorious years, and I praise You for rescuing this man, as You have rescued me."

Naturally I expected to see this man be the first one at the altar call the following Sunday, but not so. He continued as belligerent and as antagonistic as before. But there was a change in me.

It was two full years later when we were having a teaching session on loving one another, that praise swung open the door of victory. Following the teaching, we were putting our love into action by greeting one another with a hug (men with men, women with women). As I was moving among the men, I noticed my still-resentful brother trapped in a corner, an observer, not a participant. I approached him and said, "For two years I have had nothing but love for you. I have never had a chance to tell you this, but I am going to tell you now. You have blessed me more than all my friends, because you have sent me to my knees. You have made me double-check everything twice in the Word. You have caused me to worship God as no one that loves me has caused me to worship God. Because of you, I have grown in God. My brother, I love you in the Lord." With this I embraced him and kissed him on the cheek. Later that evening, during the regular service, I had the feeling that I had failed again, but I felt good in my own spirit because it had been honest. God had brought me to a place where I really did love that man.

When the service was over, a friend came and told me that this brother wanted to see me. As I stepped toward him, he turned, and I saw that tears were streaming down his face. Calling me by a nickname of former years, he said, "Little Buddy, I can't take any more of it. I am sorry it happened. Can we just bury the hatchet and be friends in Jesus again?" God welded our spirits together and gave us years of warm relationship that continues to this day.

Saints, praise is a fabulous weapon! With it we can claim and conquer and bring men to a change of heart's desire. I think it would be good if we stopped worrying about our loved ones and start praising God for their deliverance. I wonder if a lot of what we call intercession is not just an anxious mouthing of our unbelief. We do not think He heard us, so we are going to say it again. This is like the prayer wheels of China, or the water wheels of Japan, where prayers are written and attached in the belief that the prayer is prayed to the gods every time the wheel is given a spin. Once you know you have touched God in your requests, stop the petitioning and get involved in praising.

You may say, "If God has really heard, why do I not see the results?" That is because He has to answer without violating the will of the other person involved. He is having to bring him into submission through gentle channels of persuasion, and the greatest weapon you have is praise.

Do we always know whether the real enemy is men or demons? No! But God knows! If we will simply praise against all opposition, God will know against whom to move and with what level of force. "The battle is not yours, but God's" (2 Chronicles 20:15). As we continue to praise, it affords Heaven legal permission to engage in the conflict on our behalf. It is equivalent to signing a complaint or warrant against a law-breaker. Praise starts the whole legal process in motion. God is our defense. Praise Him with the highest praise you can produce, and then allow the Holy Spirit to begin a higher level of praise, that may very well lift you into the heavenlies to join the praisers up there. This will always produce a victory!

10

Preventives to Praise

In the light of all that we have seen thus far, you may well wonder why more people do not praise the Lord. I wonder if the answer, at least in part, isn't found in Romans 7:18-19, 21: "For I know that nothing good dwells within me, that is, in my flesh. I can will what is right, but I cannot perform it.— I have the intention and urge to do what is right, but no power to carry it out; For I fail to practice the good deeds I desire to do, but the evil deeds that I do not desire to do are what I am [ever] doing....So I find it to be a law [of my being] that when I want to do what is right and good, evil is ever present with me and I am subject to its insistent demands" (TAB).

Here is the great struggle and inner conflict that surfaces the moment we start to become a participant in praise. People who have been comfortable in their religion for years suddenly find themselves engaged in dissension, contention, and altercation. Even after the facts of praise are well known, the act of praise is painfully difficult. There are preventives to praise. Just what are these forces, or "laws [of my being]" (TAB), that work so possessively to prevent me from praising?

In my years of seeking to bring others into a life of praise, I have found at least seven major preventives to praise. There are undoubtedly others, but these seven seem to be the most deadly deterrents.

The first great preventive to praise, not necessarily because of its importance, but because Christians usually blame it for all negatives, is the interference of the Satanic kingdom. Having spent so many eons in service to the Kingdom of Heaven, Satan understands the value, purpose, and power of praise far better than do the people. Inasmuch as his basic purpose is to frustrate the workings of God's Kingdom, he certainly will do his utmost to restrict the flow of praise from the children to the Father. Because he knows our "high praises" can put him in bondage and immobilize his demonic forces, his first line of defense is to attack our praise before it begins and certainly before it can join the heavenly praises.

The New Testament, however, teaches that the saints are not subject to Satan, but that Satan is subject to the saints! Romans 16:20 assures us, "And the God of peace shall bruise Satan under your feet shortly." Jesus gave His disciples power and authority, over "all devils" (Luke 9:1), and assured the believers that, "In my name shall they cast out devils" (Mark 16:17).

By His life, death, Resurrection, and ascension, Jesus stripped the devil of all the power, authority, position, and rank that he had usurped and displayed before mankind. Hebrews 2:14, speaking of Jesus, says: "That through death he might destroy him that had the power of death, that is, the devil."

The Greek word translated here as "destroy," literally means to "reduce to a zero." Jesus reduced Satan to a nothing! He is a has-been. Our wonderful Lord Jesus Christ cut Satan down to the area of extremely limited power and authority he possessed in the Garden of Eden—the power of persuasion. He can only talk, entice, advertise, suggest, argue, or lie.

When Ephesians 4:27 says, "Neither give place to the devil," it sets it in a context that is discussing communication. Don't give place in your thought patterns to him. Don't talk to him, don't listen to him. Unless he has access to your mind, he is powerless to deter you from praise. He could surround you with ten thousand demons, and your praise would burn a pathway right through them. His only chance of preventing you from praising the Lord is to be able to talk you out of it, or to keep your mind so full of negative thoughts that you are unable to positively praise. Once you are fully aware of his impotence, Satan is probably the least forceful of the preventives to praise. He has no more power against you than you are willing to give him by your mental assent. "Submit yourselves therefore to God. Resist the devil, and he will flee from you" (James 4:7).

Perhaps the simple philosophy of a convert from deep sin would help those who feel the devil's intrusion into their thought patterns makes praise impossible. When asked how she could remain so victorious, she replied, "When Satan rings the doorbell, I just ask Jesus to answer the door."

A second, equally obvious preventive to praise is sin. As David so succinctly put it, "If I regard iniquity in my heart, the Lord will not hear me" (Psalm 66:18). The prophet Isaiah expressed it, "Your iniquities have separated between you and your God, and your sins have hid his face from you, that he will not hear" (Isaiah 59:2). Praise is almost impossible if the recipient rejects it, refuses it, or won't even listen to it. We are unable to handle the rejection of silence for very long. If we try to express praise to God, and the heavens seem to be "as brass," don't rebuke the devil, repent from sin. Only sin can close God's ear to your praise. We are told to "lift up holy hands" unto the Lord, not defiled hands. It is the "voice of the redeemed," that gets an audience with God, not the voice of the rebel. God wants us to "call on the Lord out of a pure heart" (2 Timothy 2:22).

Of course, we do not praise the Lord out of our own righteousness, which, in His sight, is as "filthy rags," but out of the humble righteousness of Christ, which has been conferred upon us. Sin need be no more than confessed, and it is cleansed (1 John 1:9). Sin is no problem for God, only for religion. "The blood of Jesus Christ his Son cleanseth us from all sin" (1 John 1:7). "For by one offering He hath perfected for ever them that are sanctified ... And their sins and iniquities will I remember no more" (Hebrews 10:14, 17). God dealt with sin, conclusively and eternally, at Calvary. No person need live in sin. Sin can be handled by confession and cleansing.

The Cross of Jesus deals with sin as to its penalty, its power, its presence, and its guilt.

As to sin's penalty: "Much more then, being now justified by his blood, we shall be saved from wrath through him" (Romans 5:9). "Justified," simply means just-as-if-I'd never sinned.

As to sin's power, Romans 6:14 declares, "Sin shall not have dominion over you: for ye are not under the law, but under grace." The Wesley brothers wrote and sang, "He broke the power of cancelled sin, and set the prisoner free. His blood can make the vilest clean, His blood availed for me."

As to sin's presence, God not only takes you out of "Egypt," He takes "Egypt" out of you. Immediately after Passover is the Red Sea, which will both totally destroy the enemy's power over you, and separate you forever from returning to the land from which you were delivered. 1 Peter 2:9 states "that ye should shew forth the praises of him who hath called you out of darkness into his marvellous light."

As to sin's guilt: "There is therefore now no condemnation to them which are in Christ Jesus, who walk not after the flesh, but after the Spirit" (Romans 8:1). Looking at it from God's side, confessed sin becomes remitted guilt.

None need be hindered from praise because of sin. Deal with the sin first. Don't try to cover it; expose it to God. Confess it. Let Him cleanse it and remove every trace of it from you.

Then you can praise the Lord out of purity. And you will have fresh motivation to praise!

A third preventive to praise, and one that is very strong in many Christians' lives, is guilt. If sin has not been handled, then the guilt is actual, but all too frequently, even after we have confessed the sin, we allow the guilt to linger in our consciousness. Sometimes this is the result of a weakness of faith. Instead of believing what the Word says, that we are forgiven, we believe what we feel, and we don't feel forgiven.

All of us feel the need to "do something" to remit guilt, yet the Bible declares that Jesus has already done everything necessary for the remission of sin. Once we have confessed our sin to Christ, anything further we attempt to do to remit that sin and its guilt is only a religious response. Since it produces nothing, we find it necessary to repeat it, or replace it with another act, that is even more penalizing than the first. And Satan, the accuser of the brethren, will use every argument to get us and keep us under condemnation. Every time we wring our hands over what wretched sinners we are, Satan certainly agrees, and if we are really mired in self-condemnation, we will agree with his agreeing. But finish the sentence: we are all wretched sinners, saved by grace. And who did Jesus come to save? Sinners! Praise God He did!

Not all sense of guilt is the result of a weakness of faith, however. Often it is the result of an unwillingness to forgive ourselves. We accept the truth of the Word that God has forgiven, but add, "I can never forgive myself." Are you greater than God? If He has forgiven you, why do you refuse to forgive yourself? Haven't you yet learned the great danger of an unforgiving spirit—even if you are the object of that unforgiveness? Ephesians 4:32 says, "And be ye kind one to another, tenderhearted, forgiving one another, even as God for Christ's sake hath forgiven you." Have you lost sight of the fact that you are part of this brotherhood, this Body?

Don't let your knowledge of your motivations, thought life, and dreams keep you from accepting His forgiveness, or from forgiving yourself. He knew all these inner workings when He said, "Neither do I condemn thee: go and sin no more" (John 8:11). You weren't forgiven because He didn't have all the facts. He knew, and forgave anyway. Walk out of guilt, let the shackles fall from your hands, so those hands may be lifted in praise. Get your eyes off your failures, and back onto your forgiving God, for this will motivate you to praise. Stop condemning your past; it is ruining your present, and destroying your chance for a praise-filled future.

When the Scripture promises, "if any man be in Christ, he is a new creature: old things are passed away; behold, all things are become new" (2 Corinthians 5:17), that is exactly what it means. Dare to believe it. Conduct your life as a new person. The past is canceled and buried deep; there let it lie. Concern yourself with today; grasp it, and teach it to obey your will and plan. Praise is God's command for man. Don't let a false sense of guilt frustrate the will of God for your life.

A fourth, and possibly even stronger preventive to praise, is fear—fear of ourself, fear of the opinion our peers, fear of God, fear to release inner feelings, fear of rejection, fear of ridicule, or just plain fear itself. There are few emotions in human experience that will immobilize and incapacitate a person faster than fear. Fear can stop sound reasoning, anesthetize the senses, and exercise a censorship over our will. So dangerous and so anti-God is fear that Revelation 21:8 lists "the fearful" among those who are cast into "the lake of fire." I do not believe it is so much that God is punishing them for their fear, as it is that their fear incapacitated them from entering into the promises and provisions of God. That is why Jesus, after His Resurrection, so often said, "Fear not."

I have seen people so controlled by fear that no amount of teaching on praise could move them to participate. I have watched them move all the way to the back walls of the room, withdrawing from all who were praising, as inner fear overcame conscious desire to participate in praise. Until the fear is conquered, praise is not possible. And Satan, who is the author of fear, uses it as his major weapon to counter our weapon of praise.

Like all things Satan corrupts, fear is not totally a bad thing. It is part of the defense mechanism God has built into each of us to protect us. However, it was intended to protect, not rule. There are times when we must move against our fear levels to do what we know must be done, and this is when God gives us the courage—moral, as well as physical—to overcome our natural fear and trembling. Hemingway once defined courage as "grace under stress," without ever realizing the spiritual truth he spoke.

The man who claims never to know fear is a liar. Fear is common to all of us. Often the only difference between a coward and a courageous man is the way each handled his fear. One was ruled by it, the other insisted on ruling the fear. "Lord, I know this fear is not from You. Forgive my unbelief, for doubting for an instant that You were in control of this situation, and grant me Your peace. And now, Holy Spirit, give me the words with which to praise my Maker, Defender, Redeemer, and Friend."

There is a perfect scriptural antidote to fear. "There is no fear in love; but perfect love casteth out fear: because fear hath torment. He that feareth is not made perfect in love" (1 John 4:18). The little child cries out during the night, terrorized by the thunder and lightning. The father answers, "It's all right dear; daddy's here." What kind of answer is that? It is an offering of "perfect love that casts out fear." If that answer isn't sufficient, the child is put in the bed of the parents, and feeling the warmth of love, lying next to them, he falls back to sleep in the midst of the storm.

How our heavenly Father wants to comfort the terror-stricken heart with the simple words, "It's all right now, I'm here." How His arms are outstretched to comfort and assure us of His great love! How can we fear, when so totally surrounded by His love? When a Christian gets his eyes off Satan, himself and others, and focuses the eye of his spirit upon the loving heavenly Father, his fears melt within him; he can ignore the storm that fear has produced, and respond, childlike, to a loving God whose love for him is totally perfect.

The saints of the ages, who have moved into the things of God, have learned to handle their fear by submitting it and themselves to the magnificent love of God. In the midst of the love flow, they could not be afraid.

How well I remember the deep fear levels I had to deal with in my own life, and in the lives of the people of our congregation, as we began to move into praise and worship responses to the Lord! It was during this time that a chorus, reportedly smuggled out of Communist China, came into my hands. It was said to be the "marching song of the Church in China." It had many verses, but the one I remember best is one we sang repeatedly:

"I will not be afraid. I will not be afraid,

With God beside me, His love to guide me,

I'll not be afraid!"

A fifth preventive to praise is our own ego, the attitude we have toward ourself—our self-image. Sometimes this image is extremely positive, and we see ourself as perfect, or nearly so. This type person tends to be a braggart. He is self-righteous, proud, superior, boastful, haughty, very much enamored of himself. This person has great difficulty truly praising God, for he can never seem to get his eyes completely off himself. It is hard not to pray the prayer of the publican, "God, I thank thee, that I am not as other men ..." (Luke 18:11). When he does attempt to praise, he usually expresses it as, "I praise thee that I ..."

It is very difficult to praise God, when all you can see is yourself and your accomplishments. There is a shallow form of compliment or praise that demands a response of a higher degree, but this is not acceptable praise to God. Romans 12:3 says, "For I say...to every man that is among you, not to think of himself more highly than he ought to think."

The core, the heart of praise, must be the Lord Jesus Christ. My mind must be centered upon God, not myself. My desire must be to call attention to Him, not me.

It is not only the self-exalting person, however, who has difficulty in praising. The self-abasing person has equal difficulty. Whether your attitude and expression is "How great I am" or "How worthless I am," the heart of the expression is still "I."

Some Christians never seem to get over this self-debasement. They think it is humility. They constantly speak ill of themselves, deprecate their talents and abilities, shun any service by saying they are so unworthy, and "Others can do so much better than I." The truth is, they have developed a form of self-righteousness that is far more hideous than the religious self-righteousness Paul confesses. Because it is self-deceptive, the individual is utterly, unshakably convinced of the purity of his humility. So convincing is this sham humility that the naive even point to them as examples of piety.

Nonsense! They're just as "I" centered as the braggart. In their obsequious, retiring manner, they're calling attention to themselves as surely as the person who demands the spot light. Their pride in their failures is as great as another's pride in his successes.

The same verse that warns us not to think of ourselves more highly than we ought to think, concludes, "but to think soberly, according as God hath dealt to every man the measure of faith" (Romans 12:3). We neither exalt nor abase self; we think according to what God has done for, in, and through us. What we were is not important. What we are becoming is! None among us is worthless, because the same price was paid to ransom each of us. We are to deal exclusively with God: His person, His doings, His graces, His promises, and His provisions.

Still a sixth preventive to praise involves wrong concepts of God. If we see God as harsh, tyrannical, exacting, unfeeling, or even austere, it is most difficult to release happy emotions of praise to Him. Or, if our concepts of Him are so lofty and elevated that He becomes impersonal, unapproachable, uninvolved, we again will have great difficulty worshiping with praise.

We have all picked up many of our concepts outside the Bible. We've been influenced by the way Bible stories were told to us in our childhood. We've gained many concepts from the hymns and gospel songs we have sung. The pastors under whose preaching we were taught have had a tremendous influence in molding our concepts of God. Religious art, books, movies, and dramas have determined much of our thought patterns concerning God. Our relationships with our earthly fathers obviously have an enormous influence on us.

I found it necessary to return to the Bible and find how God has revealed himself to us before my praise could be much more than an act of obedience. I needed a total new picture of the love of God, His mercy, His tender compassions, and His unfailing forgiveness. I needed to see how much He really cared, and that praise ministered to Him as well as to me.

When I began to see Him in a bridegroom relationship, as in the Song of Solomon, I found responding to Him became far more natural, and thereby, more enjoyable. I found I could respond to love, and eventually learned to respond with love. But I discovered it necessary in my case to have a "change of mind" about God, before I could accept or give Him love.

There are so many other concepts of God that will limit our praising. If we have a mental image of a God of permissiveness where everything goes because of great mercy, it will be hard to praise; all of us need and desire guidelines. Unless we see God as just, it will be difficult to praise when facing man's injustice. Unless we can see the faithfulness of God, the unfaithfulness of men may very well overwhelm us to a praiseless existence.

All we will ever know about God must come by His revelation. But that revelation has already been given to us in His Word. It is imperative that a praiser acquaint himself with the Scriptures, to increasingly enlarge his comprehension of God, that his praises unto God may abound more and more.

Perhaps a seventh preventive to praise can best be understood by reading Isaiah 61:3: "To appoint unto them that mourn in Zion, to give unto them ... the garment of praise for the spirit of heaviness; that they might be called trees of righteousness, the planting of the Lord, that he might be glorified." This seems to picture a divine exchange. He offers a "garment of praise for the spirit of heaviness." In order to be clothed with praise, we must be willing to relinquish the spirit of heaviness which has surrounded us. We must give up our self-pity, our enjoyment of our misery, and our mournful, negative attitude. Praise cannot be an addition to a negative life; it is a replacement for it! The joy replaces the sorrow. Triumphing replaces the tears. Shouting replaces the sobbing, and praise replaces the heaviness. If we have learned to be comfortable with the negatives, it may take a while to get comfortable with praise. But if you have had all of that negative, gloomy, mournful way of life you want, just hand it to the Lord, and receive, in exchange, a glorious garment of praise!

I would not presume to suggest that this list of hindrances is all-inclusive. There is the problem of the undisciplined mind that just cannot seem to keep itself focused on the Lord. Or the problem of being so out of relationship in our home that praise seems to be a mockery. But I believe these seven I have listed are major, and it is rather likely that you have seen yourself in one or more of them.

Don't bypass praise because you have something in your life that resists it. Use praise to conquer that area of your life. You'll be stronger for it, praise will flow through you like a river, God will be glorified, and the saints will, through your praise, be edified.

"Who shall separate us from the love of Christ? [Or from expressing that love?] shall tribulation, or distress, or persecution, or famine, or nakedness, or peril, or sword? ... Nay, in all these things we are more than conquerors through him that loved us. For I am persuaded, that neither death, nor life, nor angels, nor principalities, nor powers, nor things present, nor things to come, Nor height, nor depth, nor any other creature, shall be able to separate us from the love of God [or its expression], which is in Christ Jesus our Lord" (Romans 8:35, 37-39).

11

The Permanence of Praise

How wisely does the Psalmist declare, "As for man, his days are as grass: as a flower of the field, so he flourisheth. For the wind passeth over it, and it is gone; and the place thereof shall know it no more" (Psalm 103:15-16).

In our youth, our life stretched out before us as an endless pattern of opportunity, but as years advance, we become increasingly aware of the shortness of our life span. Try as we will to immortalize ourselves, life is very impermanent. Names that are in the headlines today are all but forgotten within the year. Today's heroes are often tomorrow's strangers. We are flowering grass today and fodder tomorrow. "So teach us to number our days, that we may apply our hearts unto wisdom" (Psalm 90:12).

Even the things in life over which we have control, seem to have a built-in obsolescence. The housing development, which was the pride of yesterday's generation, is demolished to make room for a freeway for this generation. Our cars, which were lauded as wonders in engineering technology when we purchased them, are often obsolete when the new model comes out.

Consider the tremendous advancement made in transportation within the lifespan of some of you older readers. From horse-and-wagon to the horseless carriage, the automobile, the train, the airplane, the jet aircraft, and now rockets to the moon and back. If that isn't almost "instant obsolescence," what is?

While all of this has brought an improvement in lifestyle, it has also brought with it a tremendous sense of impermanence, of temporization, of transience. It is difficult for the younger generation to develop any sense of permanence.

Unfortunately, religion seems to have lost much of its steadfast qualities. In the past two decades we have seen many "religious fads" come and go. There has been unbalanced emphasis upon one thing, and then another. Often the Bible has been set aside, so an "experience" could be emphasized, or a "philosophy of life" taught. In the struggle for survival, there have been many mergings that have produced conflicting compromises, leaving communicants greatly confused. There have been few authoritative declarations of "Thus saith the Lord." Whereas men used to anchor their lives to the church, now many fear that the church is sinking in the sea of change, and are loath to tie themselves to it.

We are surrounded with the carnage of death. We slaughter the population of a small city on our highways annually. We seem to be constantly engaged in a war action of one sort or another, and television has brought the horror and massacre of war into our living rooms. We hear so much of the rising tide of crimes of violence, that we have become almost hardened to it. It was recently reported that of the ten things Americans worry about the most, the first five things concern death. This report also indicated that the average American youth thinks of death once every ten minutes.

Is there anything of value that is immutable, unchangeable, enduring, or permanent to be found in our society? Is there anything we can become involved in that will not perish soon?

Yes, praise God, worship and praise are eternal and enduring by their very nature! Revelation 4:11 tells us, "Thou art worthy, O Lord, to receive glory and honour and power: for thou hast created all things, and for thy pleasure they are and were created."

This verse reveals that worship demands recognition of two things: (1) that all things come from God, and (2) all must return to God. When speaking of man, Isaiah 43:7 says, "I have created him for my glory." The man who worships and praises enters into the flow of eternity while still locked in the dimension of time. We have been created unto His pleasure, and we have already learned that it is praise that gives Him that pleasure. God's purposes for man are not temporary or limited to time, but are eternal and timeless. We are now in training for a timeless ministry! We are already engaged in eternity's highest function when we praise God. Man was made to praise the Lord, and through the work of Christ's Cross has been re-made into a creature that dares to approach a Holy God in praise.

You will remember that the shouting praise, that produced such a signal victory at Jericho, was just across the borders into the Promised Land. Far from being obsolete, praise is only the beginning revelation of what God has in store for His Church on the Earth. We are just commencing to enter into the "high praises," just at the threshold of the divine worship. This is not another religious fad that will soon pass away; praise is entering into that which God has ordained to be eternal.

In two passages in the Book of Revelation (5:8; 8:3), we see the worshipers holding vials, or censers, filled with incense which is defined as, "the prayers of the saints." The Greek word, translated here as "prayers," is also translatable as "worship." It is not simply the petitions of the saints, but their praises and worship that have ascended up before God over the ages, and have been put into incense form, and preserved in the divine presence. When the great worshipers, who stand before God's presence, begin to worship, they also present the worship of the saints on Earth. Imagine! Your praise and worship is preserved in the heavens, throughout eternity! There is something in life that is permanent, for God has chosen to preserve your praise.

Revelation 7:11-12 speaks clearly of the eternity of praising: "And all the angels stood round about the throne, and about the elders and the four beasts, and fell before the throne on their faces, and worshipped God, Saying, Amen: Blessing, and glory, and wisdom, and thanksgiving, and honour, and power, and might, be unto our God for ever and ever."

Perhaps the most arresting argument for the permanence of praise is rooted in the nature of the object of our praise. It is God we are praising. It is Jesus Christ we are worshiping, and over and over in the Book of Revelation, it speaks of "Him that sitteth upon the throne … for ever and ever" (Revelation 5:13). As long as the object of our praises exists, He will continue to excite our praise.

When we are released from the planet Earth, and ushered into God's great heavens, what an inspiration to praise will meet us. When we stand with "ten thousand times ten thousand, and thousands of thousands" of angels (Revelation 5:11), and multitudes of people, "which no man could number, of all nations, and kindreds, and people, and tongues" (Revelation 7:9), how electrifying will be our praise motivation! When all the angels of God's creating stand around God's throne, and the four living creatures (RSV) begin to lead the praise, while the twenty-four elders fall on their faces before the throne (Revelation 7:11), how could we help but be carried away in the vast spirit of worship and praise of that very hour!

And so we are able to insert a parenthesis in the midst of the eternity and interpolate our human, weak, fragile praise and know it will be incorporated forever into the worship of our heavenly Father. And since praise is eternal, it will likely take much of eternity to teach us all the truths about it. This book is just a small part of the beginning.

Appendix

Some Examples of Methods of Praise
in Scripture

Using the mouth in praise:

I heard a great voice of much people in heaven, saying, Alleluia, Salvation, and glory, and honour, and power, unto the Lord our God. (Revelation 19:1)

O sing unto the Lord a new song, for he hath done marvellous things. (Psalm 98:1)

I will worship toward thy holy temple, and praise thy name for thy lovingkindness and for thy truth. (Psalm 138:2)

Give unto the Lord the glory due unto his name. (Psalm 96:8)

I will give thee thanks in the great congregation. I will praise thee among much people (Psalm 35:18)

I will pray with the spirit, and I will pray with the understanding also; I will sing with the spirit, and I will sing with the understanding also. (1 Corinthians 14:15)

Bless the Lord. (Psalm 103:20)

O magnify the Lord with me, and let us exalt his name together. (Psalm 34:3)

Speaking to yourselves in psalms and hymns and spiritual songs, singing and making melody in your heart to the Lord. (Ephesians 5:19)

And cried with a loud voice, saying, Salvation to our God which sitteth upon the throne, and unto the Lamb. (Revelation 7:10)

Then was our mouth filled with laughter, and our tongue with singing. (Psalm 126:2)

Let them exalt him also in the congregation of the people, and praise him in the assembly of the elders. (Psalm 107:32)

And let them sacrifice the sacrifices of thanksgiving, and declare his works with rejoicing. (Psalm 107:22)

Make a joyful noise unto the Lord, all the earth: make a loud noise, and rejoice, and sing praise. (Psalm 98:4)

Let them ever shout for joy, because thou defendest them: let them also that love thy name be joyful in thee. (Psalm 5:11)

Be glad in the Lord, and rejoice, ye righteous: and shout for joy, all ye that are upright in heart. (Psalm 32:11)

I will extol thee, O Lord. (Psalm 30:1).

Let my mouth be filled with thy praise and with thy honour all the day. (Psalm 71:8)

Using the Hands in Praise

Lifting the hands:

I will lift up my hands in thy name. (Psalm 63:4)

My hands also will I lift up unto thy commandments. (Psalm 119:48)

Lift up your hands in the sanctuary, and bless the Lord. (Psalm 134:2)

The lifting up of my hands as the evening sacrifice. (Psalm 141:2)

Clapping the hands:

O clap your hands, all ye people. (Psalm 47:1)

Let the floods clap their hands. (Psalm 98:8)

All the trees of the field shall clap their hands. (Isaiah 55:12)

Playing musical instruments:

Praise the Lord with harp. (Psalm 33:2)

Awake up, my glory; awake psaltery and harp. (Psalm 57:8)

Upon a psaltery and an instrument of ten strings will I sing praises unto thee. (Psalm 144:9)

Sing praise upon the harp unto our God. (Psalm 147:7)

Praise him with the sound of the trumpet: praise him with the psaltery and harp. Praise him with the timbrel ... praise him with stringed instruments and organs. Praise him upon the loud cymbals: praise him upon the high sounding cymbals. (Psalm 150:3-5)

Using the Posture or Motion of the Body in Praise

Dancing:

Thou hast turned for me my mourning into dancing. (Psalm 30:11)

Let them praise his name in the dance. (Psalm 149:3)

Praise him with the ... dance. (Psalm 150:4)

And David danced before the Lord with all his might. (2 Sam. 6:14)

Walking and leaping:

And he leaped up, stood, and walked, and he entered with them into the temple, walking, and leaping, and praising God. (Acts 3:8)

David leaping and dancing before the Lord. (2 Sam. 6:16)

Standing:

Ye that stand in the house of the Lord. (Psalm 135:2)

Bless ye the Lord, all ye servants of the Lord, which by night stand in the house of the Lord. (Psalm 134:1)

Bowing and kneeling:

O come, let us worship and bow down: let us kneel before the Lord our maker. (Psalm 95:6)

I bow my knees unto the Father of our Lord Jesus Christ. (Ephesians 3:14)

Some Scriptures on Praise, Book by Book, through the Bible

Genesis 14:20: The praise of Melchizedek: "Blessed be the most high God, which hath delivered thine enemies into thy hand."

Genesis 29:35: The praise of Leah: "And she said, Now will I Praise the Lord: therefore she called his name Judah."

Exodus 15:1-19: The Song of Moses which will be sung in Heaven: "I will sing unto the Lord, for he hath triumphed gloriously....The Lord is my strength and song, and he is become my salvation: he is my God, and I will prepare him an habitation; my father's God, and I will exalt him.

... Thy right hand, O Lord, is become glorious in power.

... And in the greatness of thine excellency thou hast overthrown them that rose up against thee.

... Who is like unto thee, O Lord, among the gods? who is like thee, glorious in holiness, fearful in praises, doing wonders?

... The Lord shall reign for ever and ever."

Leviticus 19:24: "The fruit ... shall be holy to praise the Lord withal."

Numbers 21:16-17: "The Lord spake unto Moses, Gather the people together, and I will give them water. Then Israel sang this song, Spring up, O well; sing ye unto it."

Deuteronomy 10:21: "He is thy praise, and he is thy God ... "

Joshua 6:20: The praiseful shouting at Jericho's walls: "When the people heard the sound of the trumpet, and the people shouted with a great shout, ... the wall fell down flat."

Judges 5:2-3: The praise of Deborah and Barak: "Praise ye the Lord for the avenging of Israel, when the people willingly offered themselves. Hear, O ye kings; give ear, O ye princes; I, even I will sing unto the Lord; I will sing praise to the Lord God of Israel."

Ruth 4:14: "And the women said unto Naomi, Blessed be the Lord, which hath not left thee this day without a kinsman, that his name may be famous in Israel."

1 Samuel 2:1-2: "And Hannah prayed, and said, My heart rejoiceth in the Lord, mine horn is exalted in the Lord.

... There is none holy as the Lord: for there is none beside thee: neither is there any rock like our God."

2 Samuel 22:4: The praise of David after his deliverance from Saul: "I will call on the Lord who is worthy to be praised."

1 Kings 8:15: Solomon's praise of God at the dedication of the Temple: "Blessed be the Lord God of Israel, which spake with his mouth unto David my father, and hath with his hand fulfilled it."

2 Kings 3:15-16: The singing praise of a minstrel stirred the prophetic gift in Elisha: "And it came to pass, when the minstrel played, that the hand of the Lord came upon him. And he said, Thus saith the Lord ..."

1 Chronicles 16:4: "And he [David] appointed certain of the Levites ... to thank and praise the Lord God of Israel."

2 Chronicles 20:21: Tells of Jehoshaphat's praising choir: "He appointed singers unto the Lord ... that should praise the beauty of holiness ... and ... say, Praise the Lord; for his mercy endureth forever."

Ezra 3:11: Speaks of the loud shouting praise at the foundation laying of the Temple: "And they sang together by course in praising and giving thanks unto the Lord; because he is good, and his mercy endureth forever toward Israel. And all the people shouted with a great shout, when they praised the Lord, because the foundation of the house of the Lord was laid."

Nehemiah 12:24: Tells of praisers being re-appointed to the service of the Lord: "And the chief of the Levites: Hashabiah, Sherebiah, and Jeshua the son of Kadmiel, with their brethren over against them, to praise and to give thanks, according to the commandment of David, the man of God."

Esther 8:15-16: Gives the praise of the Jews at Shushan after divine intervention had saved Mordecai: "And the city of Shushan rejoiced and was glad. The Jews had light, and gladness, and joy, and honour."

Job 13:15: Praises in the midst of negatives: "Though He slay me, yet will I trust in him."

Psalms lists the praises of David, Solomon, Asaph, Sons of Korah, and others.

Proverbs 8:30-31: "I was daily his delight, rejoicing always before him; Rejoicing in the habitable part of his earth."

Ecclesiastes 2:26; 3:12, 22: "God giveth to a man ... joy." "But for a man to rejoice." "A man should rejoice."

Song of Solomon 1:4: "Draw me, we will run after thee: the king hath brought me into his chambers: we will be glad and rejoice in thee."

Isaiah 43:21: "This people have I formed for myself; they shall shew forth my praise:"

Jeremiah 33:11: "The voice of joy, and the voice of gladness ... the voice of them that shall say, Praise the Lord of hosts ... and of them that shall bring the sacrifice of praise into the house of the Lord."

Lamentations 3:41: "Let us lift up our heart with our hands unto God in the heavens."

Ezekiel 44:15: Shows the specified priests who shall minister directly to the Lord: "But the priests the Levites, the sons of Zadok, that kept the charge of my sanctuary when the children of Israel went astray from me, they shall come near to me to minister unto me, and they shall stand before me to offer unto me the fat and the blood, saith the Lord God."

Daniel 2:20: "Blessed be the name of God for ever and ever: for wisdom and might are his."

Hosea 12:6: "Wait on thy God continually." (Compare with Psalm 65:1: "Praise waiteth for thee, O God.")

Joel 2:23: "Be glad then, ye children of Zion, and rejoice in the Lord your God."

Amos 9:11: "In that day will I raise up the tabernacle of David that is fallen."

Obadiah 1:17: "But upon mount Zion shall be deliverance, and there shall be holiness." (As we see this last day "revival" being fulfilled, we find praise as its keynote.)

Jonah 2:9: "I will sacrifice unto thee with the voice of thanksgiving."

Micah 7:7-9: "Therefore I will look unto the Lord; I will wait for the God of my salvation: my God will hear me." (Read the next two verses.)

Nahum 1:15: "Behold upon the mountains the feet of him that bringeth good tidings, that publisheth peace! O Judah [which means Praise], keep thy solemn feasts, perform thy vows."

Habakkuk 3:18: "Yet I will rejoice in the Lord, I will joy in the God of my salvation."

Zephaniah 3:14: "Sing, O daughter of Zion; shout, O Israel; be glad and rejoice with all the heart, O daughter of Jerusalem."

Haggai 2:7, 9: God promises to give greater glory to the second Temple: "I will fill this house with glory, saith the Lord of hosts ... The glory of this latter house shall be greater than of the former."

Zechariah 9:9: The "Palm Sunday" prophecy, "Rejoice greatly, O daughter of Zion; shout O daughter of Jerusalem: behold, thy King cometh unto thee: he is just, and having salvation; lowly, and riding upon an ass."

Malachi 1:5: "And your eyes shall see, and ye shall say, The Lord will be magnified."

Matthew 26:30: Jesus and the disciples at the time of His Passion: "And when they had sung an hymn, they went out into the mount of Olives."

Mark 11:8-10: Describes Palm Sunday with the rejoicing of the people: "And many spread their garments in the way: and others cut down branches off the trees, and strawed them in the way. And they that went before, and they that followed, cried, saying, Hosanna; Blessed is he that cometh in the name of the Lord: Blessed be the kingdom of our father David, that cometh in the name of the Lord."

Luke 1:46-55: Gives Mary's glorious Magnificat of praise: "My soul doth magnify the Lord, And my spirit hath rejoiced in God my Saviour …

John 1:49: Nathanael praises Jesus, saying, "Rabbi, thou art the Son of God; thou art the King of Israel."

John 7:37-39: Tells of the flow of the Holy Spirit that produces praise: "Jesus stood and cried, saying, If any man thirst, let him come unto me, and drink. He that believeth on me, as the scripture hath said, out of his belly shall flow rivers of living water. (But this spake he of the Spirit, which they that believe on him should receive.)

Acts 16:25: In prison, "At midnight Paul and Silas prayed, and sang praises unto God."

Romans 15:11: "Praise the Lord, all ye Gentiles; and laud him, all ye people."

1 Corinthians 14:15: "I will pray with the spirit … I will sing with the spirit."

2 Corinthians 8:18: "Whose praise is in the gospel throughout all the churches."

Galatians 4:27: "For it is written, Rejoice, thou barren that bearest not; break forth and cry."

Ephesians 1:12: "That we should be to the praise of his glory, who first trusted in Christ."

Philippians 4:20: "Now unto God and our Father be glory for ever and ever. Amen."

Colossians 1:3: "We give thanks to God and the Father of our Lord Jesus Christ."

1 Thessalonians 5:16: "Rejoice evermore."

2 Thessalonians 1:3: "We are bound to thank God always for you."

1 Timothy 2:8: "I will therefore that men pray everywhere, lifting up holy hands."

2 Timothy 4:18: "And the Lord shall deliver me ... to whom be glory for ever and ever."

Titus makes no mention of praise, but abundant reasons for praise are given, and we know the author was a praiser.

Philemon 4: "I thank my God, making mention of thee always in my prayers."

Hebrews 2:12: "Saying, I will declare thy name unto my brethren, in the midst of the church will I sing praise unto thee.

James 5:13: "Is any merry? let him sing psalms."

1 Peter 1:7: "That the trial of your faith ... might be found unto praise and honour and glory at the appearing of Jesus Christ."

2 Peter 1:5: "Add to your faith virtue" (Greek arete, translated in 1 Peter 2:9 as "praises").

1 John 4:17: "Because as He is, so are we in this world." Jesus was a praiser—so are we.

2 John 4: "I rejoiced greatly that I found of thy children walking in truth."

3 John 3: "I rejoiced greatly, when the brethren came and testified of the truth that is in thee, even as thou walkest in the truth."

Jude 24-25: "Now unto Him that is able to keep you from falling, and to present you faultless before the presence of his glory with exceeding joy, To the only wise God our Saviour, be glory and majesty, dominion and power, both now and ever. Amen."

Revelation 19:5: "And a voice came out of the throne, saying, Praise our God, all ye his servants, and ye that fear him, both small and great."

Scriptures Concerning Praising in the Congregation

Psalm 22:22: "I will declare thy name unto my brethren: in the midst of the congregation will I praise thee."

Psalm 22:25: "My praise shall be of thee in the great congregation: I will pay my vows before them that fear him."

Psalm 111:1: "Praise ye the Lord. I will praise the Lord with my whole heart, in the assembly of the upright, and in the congregation."

Psalm 149:1: "Praise ye the Lord. Sing unto the Lord a new song, and his praise in the congregation of saints."

1 Chronicles 29:20: "And all the congregation blessed the Lord God of their fathers, and bowed down their heads, and worshipped the Lord."

2 Chronicles 29:28: "And all the congregation worshipped, and the singers sang, and the trumpeters sounded: and all this continued until the burnt offering was finished."

Psalm 35:18: "I will give thee thanks in the great congregation:I will praise thee among much people."

Psalm 26:12: "My foot standeth in an even place: in the congregations will I bless the Lord."

Psalm 68:26: "Bless ye God in the congregations, even the Lord."

1 Peter 2:9: "But ye are a chosen generation, a royal priesthood, an holy nation, a peculiar people; that ye should shew forth the praises of him who hath called you out of darkness into his marvellous light."

Devil-Demons

The following is quoted from the Expository Dictionary of New Testament Words by W.E. Vine, published by Fleming H. Revell Company:

Devil, devilish (from page 306)

Diabolos, an accuser, a slanderer, is one of the names of Satan. From it the English word "Devil" is derived, and should be applied only to Satan, as a proper name. Diamön, a demon, is frequently, but wrongly, translated "devil," it should always be translated "demon," as in the R.V. margin. There is one Devil, there are many demons. Being the malignant enemy of God and man, he accuses man to God, Job 1:6-11; 2:1-5; Rev. 12:9, 10, and God to man, Gen. 3. Being himself sinful, 1 John 3:8, he instigated man to sin, Gen. 3, and tempts man to do evil, Eph. 4:27; 6:11 encouraging him thereto by deception, Eph. 2:2.

Demon, demoniac (from page 291)

Daimön, a demon ... In the N.T. it denotes an evil spirit. It is used in Matt. 8:31, mistranslated "devils."

Daimonion,. . .the neuter of the adjective daimonios, pertaining to a demon, is also mistranslated "devil," "devils." ...Demons are the spiritual agents acting in all idolatry. The idol itself is nothing, but every idol has a demon associated with it who introduces idolatry, with its worship and sacrifices, 1 Cor. 10:20, 21; Rev. 9:20; cp. Deut. 32:17; Isa. 13:21; 34:14; 65:3, 11. They disseminate errors among men, and seek to seduce believers, 1 Tim. 4:1. As seducing spirits they deceive men into the supposition that through mediums (those who have "familiar spirits," Lev. 20:6, 27 e.g.) they can converse with deceased human beings. Hence the destructive deception of Spiritism, forbidden in Scripture, Lev. 19:31; Deut. 18:11; Isa. 8:19. Demons tremble before God, Jas. 2:19; they recognized Christ as Lord and as their future Judge, Matt. 8:29; Luke 4:41. Christ cast them out of human beings by His own power. His disciples did so in His Name, and by exercising faith, e.g. Matt. 17:20.

Acting under Satan (cp. Rev. 16:13, 14) demons are permitted to afflict with bodily disease, Luke 13:16. Being unclean they tempt human beings with unclean thoughts, Matt. 10: 1; Mark 5:2, 7:25; Luke 8:27-29; Rev. 16:13; 18:2, e.g. They differ in degrees of wickedness, Matt. 12:45. They will instigate the rulers of the nations at the end of this age to make war against God and His Christ, Rev. 16:14.

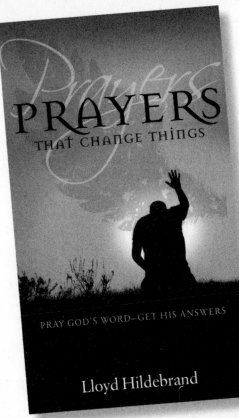

Prayers That Change Things
Pray God's Word— Get His Answers
by Lloyd Hildebrand

Prayers That
Change Things
is a new book by an
established writer
of books on prayer,
Lloyd B. Hildebrand,
who co-authored the
very popular *Prayers
That Prevail* series,
*Bible Prayers for All
Your Needs*, *Praying
the Psalms*, *Healing
Prayers*, and several
others. This new
book contains
prayers about personal feelings
and situations, prayers that are built directly from the Bible.
The reader will discover that praying the Scriptures will truly bring
about changes to so many things, especially their outlook on life
and the circumstances of life. These life-imparting, life-generating,
life-giving, and life-sustaining prayers are sure to bring God's
answers to meet the believer's needs. Pray them from your heart;
then wait for God to speak to you. Remember, He always speaks
through His Word.

This revolutionary approach joins the power of prayer with the
power of God's Word.

ISBN: 978-1-61036-105-7
MM / 192 pages

"The Consummate Apologetics Bible...

Everything you ever need to share your faith."

"The Evidence Bible is the reservoir overflowing with everything evangelistic—powerful quotes from famous people, amazing anecdotes, sobering last words, informative charts, and a wealth of irrefutable evidence to equip, encourage, and enlighten you, like nothing else.

I couldn't recommend it more highly."
– Kirk Cameron

Compiled by Ray Comfort

This edition of *The Evidence Bible* includes notes, commentaries, and quotations that make it a comprehensive work of apologetics and evangelism that will be helpful to every believer. It covers a variety of practical topics, including the following:

- How to answer objections to Christianity
- How to talk about Christ with people of other religions
- How to counter evolutionary theories, while providing evidence for God's creation
- How to grow in Christ
- How to use the Ten Commandments when witnessing

There is no other Bible like this one. Every soul-winner who wants to lead others to Christ will want a copy of *The Evidence Bible*, because it provides springboards for preaching and witnessing, shares insights from well-known Christian leaders, gives points for open-air preaching, reveals the scientific facts contained within the Bible, and supplies the believer with helpful keys to sharing one's faith. The Bible is "the sword of the Spirit," and this edition of the Bible will motivate believers to become true spiritual warriors in their daily interactions with others.

THE
EVIDENCE
BIBLE NKJV

All You Need to Understand and Defend Your Faith

IN THE BEGINNING
GOD CREATED THE
HEAVENS AND THE
EARTH AND THE
EARTH WAS

COMMENTARY BY
RAY COMFORT

ISBN: 9780882705255
PB

*Also available in
duo tone leather.*

ISBN: 9780882708973

The
Evidence
Bible Irrefutable
evidence
for the
thinking mind

King James Version
New Testament,
Psalms and
Proverbs

THE WAY OF THE MASTER
W D J D
MARK 16:15

Compiled by
Ray Comfort

Prove God's existence.

Answer 100 common objections to Christianity.

Show the Bible's supernatural origin.

Bridge Logos

Top 20

Pure Gold Classics
Timeless Truth in a Distinctive, Best-Selling Collection

- Illustrations
- Detailed index
- Author biography
- In-depth Bible study
- Expanding Collection—40-plus titles
- Sensitively Revised in Modern English

AN EXPANDING COLLECTION
OF THE BEST-LOVED
CHRISTIAN CLASSICS
OF ALL TIME.

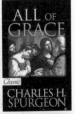

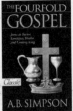
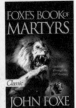

AVAILABLE AT FINE BOOKSTORES.
FOR MORE INFORMATION,
VISIT WWW.BRIDGELOGOS.COM

 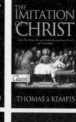 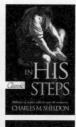 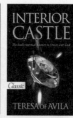

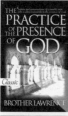 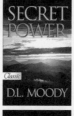   

 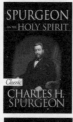   

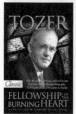   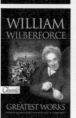 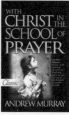